WILMETTE PUBLIC LIBRARY
3 1239 00419 7692

MEL BAY PRESENTS

SONGS OF GERMANY

DEUTSCHE LIEDER

D0927724

By
Jerry
Silverman

MEL BAY

Visit us on the Web at http://www.melbay.com — E-mail us at email@melbay.com

Contents

Introduction

Approximately since the 15th Century and, particularly, since the invention of printed musical notation a hundred years later, an ever-increasing number of German folksongs have been collected and preserved. Many of them express the "voice of the people" in its needs and struggles — a voice that by the 19th Century was groaning under bondage and was echoed in the countryside in uprisings of impoverished farmers; in the cities by struggling artisans and the poor against the patrician ruling class; and later by the newly rising working class.

Many of these songs reflect the traditional German love of wandering and nature. Songs of the open road abound, but these are not always "escapist" in nature. They deal with the harsh realities of life in difficult circumstances, and the hope for a better life somewhere else. Indeed, in this respect they foreshadow the pioneer songs of the American frontier and the later Okie ballads of our own Woody Guthrie (not least for their utter contempt for the powers-that-be, and their saucy thumbing of the nose at the Establishment).

Indeed, it was only natural that this footloose spirit should have led to the ultimate adventure (in the 19th Century): emigration to America. And so, out of the wandering musician, tinker and adventurer of the Middle Ages emerged a new breed of wanderer who set off across the ocean into the unknown.

This collection includes songs like "Der Bettelvogt" (The Bailiff), from those early pre-industrial days, and contains student songs, drinking songs, songs of love, wanderlust, discontent and leave-taking (including emigration) throughout the years, concluding with "Die Moorsoldaten" (The Peat-Bog Soldiers), a concentration-camp song of the 1930s.

The songs have been chosen for their historical as well as musical interest. I hope you enjoy them!

Jerry Silverman

Those of you who will sing these songs in German will come across a number of odd-looking spellings, words and songs. In some cases footnotes have been included to give the modern German equivalents of these antique or folksy words.

Als wir jüngst in Regensburg waren
When We Were In Regensburg Lately

The old city of Regensburg is in Bavaria, between Munich and Nuremburg, at the confluence of the Danube and Regen rivers. The waters are particularly turbulent at this point, hence, the references to the "whirlpool" in this song.

C G7 C
Als wir jüngst in Re - gens - burg wa - ren, sind wir ü - ber den
When we were in Re - gens - burg late - ly, we passed o - ver the
G7 C F C
Stru - del ge - fah - ren. Da war'n vie - le Hol - den,
whirl - pool safe - ly, There the pret - ty wo - men
G7 C G7 C Chorus C7
die mit - fah - ren woll - ten. Schwä - bi - sche, bay - ri - sche
were all read - y to plunge in. Swa - bian, Ba - va - ri - an
F C G7 C G7 C
Dirn - del, juch - hei - ras - sa, muß der Schiffs - man fah - ren.
la - dies, just look at them, Boat - man, bring them o - ver.

Und vom hohen Bergesschlosse
kam auf stolzem, schwarzem Rosse
adlig Fräulein Kunigund,
wollt' mitfahren über Strudels Grund. *(Chorus)*

›› Schiffsmann, lieber Schiffsmann mein,
soll's denn so gefährlich sein?
Schiffsmann, sag' mir's ehrlich,
ist's denn so gefährlich? ‹‹ *(Chorus)*

Wem der Myrtenkranz geblieben,
landet froh und sicher drüben.
Wer ihn hat verloren,
ist dem Tod erkoren. *(Chorus)*

Als sie auf die Mitt' gekommen,
kam ein großer Nix geschwommen,
nahm das Fräulein Kunigund,
fuhr mit ihr in Strudels Grund. *(Chorus)*

Und ein Mädel von zwölf Jahren
ist mit über den Strudel gefahren.
Weil sie noch nicht lieben kunnt,
fuhr sie sicher über Strudels Grund. *(Chorus)*

From her mountain castle riding
On a sturdy, pitch-black horse arriving,
Noble Fraulein Konigund came down,
To cross the whirlpool into town. *(Chorus)*

Boatman, oh, my boatman dear,
Should it be so dangerous here?
Tell me truly, boatman,
What could be the problem. *(Chorus)*

He who keeps the myrtle garland,
Safely makes it to the dry land.
But he who has lost it,
Is by death accosted. *(Chorus)*

When at mid-stream she was splashing,
A big water-sprite came thrashing.
Seizing Fraulein Konigund,
To the whirlpool she was bound. *(Chorus)*

And a twelve-year-old girl coming from school,
Passed right over the mighty whirlpool.
Since for making love she wasn't yet ready,
She passed safely through the deadly eddy. *(Chorus)*

Das Schnäpsen
The Little Schnaps

The German word *Schnaps* has entered the English language as a familiar, non-specific term for a variety of strong alcoholic spirits, such as brandy, gin or whisky. You pays your money and you takes your choice.

G C G C G
Wenn ich des mor - gens früh auf - steh und muß zur Ar - beit
When in the morn - ings I get up, And off to work I
D7 G D7 G G7 C G G7 C G
ge - hen, dann kocht mir mei - ne Mut - ter Tee, von dem ich kei - nen
hast - en, Then moth - er serves me a tea cup, But I don't ev - er
D7 G *Chorus* D7 G Em7 D7 G G7
neh - me: Ich muß e Schnäps - che han, ist das nicht fein!
taste it. I need a glass of schnaps, now ain't that fine!

C
Em6
D7
G
D7
G
1.
2.
Nur noch Brann-te-wein, nur noch Schnaps! Ich muß e Schnaps!
Just some bran-dy-wine, Just some schnaps! I need a schnaps!

Und wenn ich krank geworden bin
und muß zum Doktor gehen,
verschreibt mir jener Medizin,
von der ich keine nehme: *(Chorus)*

Und wenn ich dann gestorben bin,
so sollt ihr mich begraben
in einem Faß voll Branntewein
darinnen ich mich labe.
(Chorus) Denn erst nach sechs und sechzig Liter Branntewein
schlaf ich selig ein, schlaf ich ein.

Und komm ich dann zur Himmelstür,
so tät der Petrus fragen:
›› Was willst du, Schnaps, Wein oder Bier? ‹‹
So tät ich Branntwein sagen. *(Chorus)*

And if I happen to fall ill,
Prescription's sure to follow.
The doctor says, "Just take this pill"
Which I will never swallow. *(Chorus)*

And then some day when I do die,
Just place my body gently
In a barrel full of brandywine,
And I will rest contently.
(Chorus) In sixty-six liters of brandywine,
I'll sleep so fine, I'll sleep so fine.

When I to Heaven's Gate draw near,
Saint Peter then will wonder.
"Do you want schnaps, or wine, or beer?"
"Some brandywine!" I'll thunder. *(Chorus)*

Der arme Schwartenhals
The Poor Wandering Beggar

In the 16th Century, wandering beggars *cum* highwaymen were not held in high regard in Germany (or anywhere else). They were called *Schwartenhals,* an uncomplimentary term derived from *Schwarte* (bacon rind or pigskin) and *Hals* (neck), because of their open collars and generally unsavory appearance. The term was also applied derisively to infantry soldiers *(Landsknecht),* whose presence in France during this period is the linguistic source for the French equivalent, *lancequenet.*

Em D G
Ich kam vor einer Frau Wir - tin Haus, man
I come to a land - la - dy's inn, They
D7 G D7 Em B7 Em Bm Em
fragt mich, wer ich wä – re? Ich bin ein ar - mer
all do take my mea – sure. I am just a poor
C Am B D7 G Am6 Em Bm Em
Schwar - ten - hals, ich äß und tränk so ger - ne.
sim - ple guy, I eat and drink with plea - sure.

Man führt mich in die Stuben ein,
da gab man mir zu trinken,
mein Augen ließ ich umhergan,
den Becher ließ ich sinken.

Man setzt mich oben an den Tisch,
als ich ein Kaufherr wäre,
und da es an ein Zahlen ging,
mein Säckel stund mir leere.

Da ich zu nachts wollt schlafen gan,
man wies mich in die Scheuer,
da wart mir armen Schwartenhals
mein Lachen viel zu teuer.

Und da ich in die Scheuer kam,
da hub ich an zu nisten,
da stachen mich die Hagedorn,
dazu die rauhen Distel.

Da ich des morgens früh aufstund,
der Reif lag auf dem Dache,
da muß ich armer Schwartenhals
meins Unglücks selber lachen.

Ich nahm mein Schwert wohl in die hand
und gürt es an die Seiten,
ich armer muß zu Füßen gan,
das macht: ich hat nit z'reiten.

Ich hub mich auf und ging davon,
und macht mich auf die Straßen;
mir kam eins reichen Kaufmanns Sohn:
sein Tasch' mußt er mir lassen.

They lead me to the dining room,
And drink, they give me plenty.
My eyes are looking everywhere,
My cup, it falls down empty.

The table then for me is set,
As if I were a merchant.
And when it's time to pay the bill,
My purse does not have one cent.

And when I want to go to sleep,
It's to the barn they steer me.
Into the empty barn I creep,
I laugh, but they don't hear me.

And so I come into the barn,
I lie down on my straw bed,
Where I am stuck by the hawthorne,
And thistles pick me raw red.

And in the morning when I woke,
The frost lay on the rooftop.
I laughed, poor beggar, at the joke,
Of how my life was goofed up.

I take my sword all in my hand,
Around my waist it's tied on.
But, poor me, I must go on foot,
I have no horse to ride on.

So I get up and I go out,
And head straight for the highway,
Where I meet a rich merchant's son
His purse, it must come my way.

Wir haben drei Katzen
We Have Three Cats

D G A7 D 1.
Wir ha - ben drei Kat - zen, fängt kei - ne kein' Maus; wir
ha - ben drei Jung - fern, sieht kei - ne schön
O, we have three cats, but not one can catch mice; And
we have three vir - gins, they don't look so
2. D G D G D Em E7 A7sus4 A7
aus; Wir ha - ben drei Kut - scher, kann kei - ner nicht fahrn; Wir
nice. And we have three coach - men, they drive with - out rules, And
D G G♯dim A7 Bm6 A7 D
ha - ben drei Dok - torn, sind al - le drei narrn.
we have three doc - tors, they're each of them fools.

Wir haben drei Pfannen, hat keine kein' Stiel;
wir haben drei Müller, hat keiner kein' Mühl;
wir haben drei Patres, hat keiner kein Kind;
wir haben drei Ochsen, war keiner kein Rind.

Wir haben drei Kranke, tut keinem nichts weh;
wir haben drei Töchter, kommt keine zur Eh';
wir haben drei Hennen, legt keine kein Ei;
wir haben drei Hahnen, tut keiner kein' Schrei.

Wir haben drei Schneider, macht keiner kein Kleid;
wir haben drei Geigen, hat keine kein' Sait;
wir haben drei Messer, hat keines kein' Spitz;
wir haben drei Feuer, hat keines kein' Hitz.

Oh, we have three skillets, but handles they've nil;
And we have three millers, not one has a mill;
And we have three fathers with not a child born;
And we have three oxen, not one has a horn.

Oh, we have three patients, they don't stay in bed;
And we have three daughters, not one of them's wed;
And we have three hens, but no eggs do they lay;
And we have three roosters, they don't crow for day.

Oh, we have three tailors, they don't sew a thing;
And we have three fiddles, not one has a string;
And we have three knives, but not one can cut meat;
And we have three fires, but not one does give heat.

Ich fahr dahin
I Ride Away

D7 G D D7 G D Em
Ich fahr da - hin, wann es muß sein; ich
The time has come, I ride a - way, I
D A7 D Bm6 A7 D G D7 G G7
scheid mich von der Lieb - sten mein, Zur Letzt laß ich das
tell my love I can - not stay. My heart re - mains as
C B Em G Am G C C♯dim G B Em D
Her - ze mein, die - weil ich leb; so soll es sein.
I do go; while I'm a - live, it must be so.
G D Em C G Em D7 G
Ich fahr da - hin, ich fahr da - hin.
I ride a - way, I ride a - way.

Das sag ich ihr und niemand meh:
Mei'm Herzen g'schah noch nie so weh;
sie g'liebet mir je läng'r je mehr.
Durch Meiden muß ich leiden Pein.
Ich fahr dahin, ich fahr dahin.

Halt deine Treu so stet als ich!
Wie du wilt, so findest du mich.
Halt dich in Hut! Das bitt ich dich.
Geseg'n dich Gott! Ich fahr dahin,
Ich fahr dahin, ich fahr dahin.

I tell her only she can know,
My heart is suffering such woe.
She loves me truly, though in vain.
In fleeing I must suffer pain.
I ride away, I ride away.

Don't grieve for me, as I for you,
For if you will, you'll find me true.
Take care, take care, is all I say,
May God bless you! I ride away.
I ride away, I ride away.

Zur Letzt: Zum Abschied

Mädchenkunde eines Fahrenden
Young-Woman Wisdom Of A Traveling Musician

A reference to this song, dated Agdorf, 1460, informs us: "This streetsinger's song lets us know that in those days, the young women in Franconia distinguished themselves because of their pretty figures; in Swabia, because of their spinning; in the Rhineland, because of their love of singing; in Bavaria, because of their cooking skills; in Lower Saxony, because of their full barns and cultivation of flax...." Flax threshing and having a big flail, etc., are unmistakable erotic references, with their equivalents found in songs of many other countries.

C Am Em C7 F
Ich spring an die - sem Rin - ge, des be - sten so ich's
hüb - schen Fräu - lein sin - gen, als ich's ge - ler - net
I spring in - to the dance now, The best way that I
sing of pret - ty la - dies, As I have learned to
1. 2.
C C G F G7 C Am
kann, von han. Ich ritt durch frem - de Lan - de, da
know, And do. Through for - eign lands I've rid - den, where
Em Dm C G7 C Am G7 C
sah ich man - cher - han - de, da ich die Fräu - lein fand.
girls are nev - er hid - den, I've met them as I go.

Die Fräuwelein von Franken,
die seh ich allzeit gern;
nach ihn 'stehn mein' Gedanken,
sie geben süßen Kern.
Sie sein die feinsten Dirnen,
wollt Gott, ich sollt ihn' zwirnen,
spinnen wollt ich lern!

The pretty Frankish women,
That I do love to see,
My thoughts are always with 'em,
They are so good to me.
They simply are the finest,
I'd twine them into my nest,
If I could spin, you see.

Die Fräuwelein von Schwaben,
die haben golden Haar,
sie dürfen's frischlich wagen,
sie spinnen über lar;
wer ihn' den Flachs will schwingen,
der muß sein nit geringe,
das sag ich euch fürwahr.

The pretty girls from Swabia,
They have such golden hair,
You have to venture boldly,
As they spin over there.
If flax you would be flailing.
Then get there without failing.
I tell you that for sure.

Die Fräuwelein vom Rheine,
die lob ich oft und dick:
sie sind hübsch und feine
und geben freundlich Blick.
Sie können Seiden spinnen,
die neuen Liedlein singen,
sie seind der Lieb ein Strick.

The lovely Rhenish maidens,
I praise them far and wide.
They are so nice and pretty.
With friendly looks beside.
The silk threads they are spinning,
The latest songs are singing.
They'd make a lovely bride.

Die Fräuwelein von Sachsen,
die haben Scheuern weit,
darin da poßt man Flachse,
der in der Scheuren leit.
Wer ihn' den Flachs will possen,
muß habn' ein Flegel große,
dreschend zu aller Zeit.

The Saxon girls are something,
Their barns are big and wide.
Their flax it gets a threshing,
The flax that is inside.
If flax threshing's your pleasure,
Your flail must really measure,
And thresh from side to side.

Die Fräuwelein von Bayern,
die können kochen wohl,
mit Käsen und mit Eiern
ihr Küchen die sind voll.
Sie haben schöne Pfannen,
weiter dann die Wannen,
heißer denn ein Kohl.

Bavaria's sweet ladies,
They sure know how to cook
With cheeses and with eggs,
They're really worth a look.
Their pans cook up the best grub,
They're wider than a bath tub.
Those ladies wrote the book.

Den Fräuwelein soll man hofieren
allzeit, und weil man mag,
die Zeit, die kummet schiere,
es wird sich alle Tag.
Nun bin ich worden alte,
zum Wein muß ich mich halten,
alldieweil ich mag.

So always court the ladies,
Just as long as you can,
For time is growing short now,
I'm sure you understand.
As I grow old I'm thinking,
That wine I must keep drinking,
All the while I can.

an diesem Ringe	der Reigen, der gesprungen wurde
possen	klopfen, dreschen
es wird sich alle Tag	es reiht sich Tag an Tag

Die Blätter von den Bäumen
The Leaves From All The Green Trees

G
A7
Die Blät - ter von den Bäu - men, die fal - len all auf
The leaves from all the green trees Fall on me fast and
D7
1.
D7
2.
G
G/F♯
mich. Die mich. Weil mich mein Schatz ver - las -
thick. The thick. And be - cause my love has
G7/F
E+7
Am
Am/G♯
Am7/G
D/F♯
sen hat, weil mich mein Schatz ver - las - sen hat, das
gone a - way, And be - cause my love has gone a - way, It
Em
D7
G
D7
G
1.
2.
krän - ket, krän - ket mich. Das mich.
makes me ve - ry sick. It sick.

Ins Kloster will sie gehen,
will werden eine Nonn.] 2
So muß ich die Welt durchreisen,
bis daß ich zu ihr komm.] 2

Im Kloster angekommen,
ganz leise klopft ich an:] 2
›› Gebt heraus die jüngste Nonne,
die zuletzt ins Kloster kam. ‹‹] 2

›› Ist keine reingekommen,
es kommt auch keine raus;] 2
denn wer drin ist, muß drin bleiben,
im schönen Nonnenhaus. ‹‹] 2

Sie stand wohl unter der Türe,
schneeweiß war sie gekleidt;] 2
ihr Haar war abgeschnitten,
zur Nonn war sie bereit.] 2

Was trug sie unter der Schürze?
Zwei Flaschen roten Wein:] 2
›› Nimm sie hin, Herzallerliebster,
das soll dein Abschied sein. ‹‹] 2

She's entering a cloister,
She wants to be a nun,] 2
So I must travel the wide world,
Till unto her I come.] 2

I came up to the cloister,
And knocked upon the gate.] 2
"Oh, please release the youngest nun,
Who came to you of late."] 2

"No one has entered in here,
And none comes out, you see.] 2
Whoever's here, remains within,
In our fair nunnery."] 2

She's standing in the doorway,
And snow-white were her clothes.] 2
Her hair was cropped close to her head,
All ready for her vows.] 2

What have you 'neath your apron?
Two flasks of dark red wine.] 2
"Take them with you, my dearest love,
'Twill be our parting sign"] 2

Wanderlied der Prager Studenten
Wandering Song Of The Prague Students

This French hunting melody was originally played on hunting horns. German (and European) university students delighted in inserting Latin phrases (fractured or otherwise) into their songs.

Words by Joseph von Eichendorf

Music from a French hunting tune

D
A7
D
A7
D
1.
Nach Sü - den nun _ sich len - ken die Vög - lein all - zu - mal. Viel'
Wan - drer lu - stig schwen - ken die Hüt' im Mor - gen -
O, south - ward now _ are turn - ing The birds all in _ their flight. And
wan - der - ers _ are burn - ing To part at morn - ing
D
2.
A7
D
strahl. Das _ sind die Herrn _ stu - den - ten, zum Tor hin - aus _ es
light. They _ are the gen - tle - men stu - dents, Who from the gate _ do
A
D
A7
D
A7
geht, auf _ ih - ren In _ stru - men - ten sie bla - sen zum _ Va -
go. To _ sig - nal their _ de - par - ture, They give their horns _ a

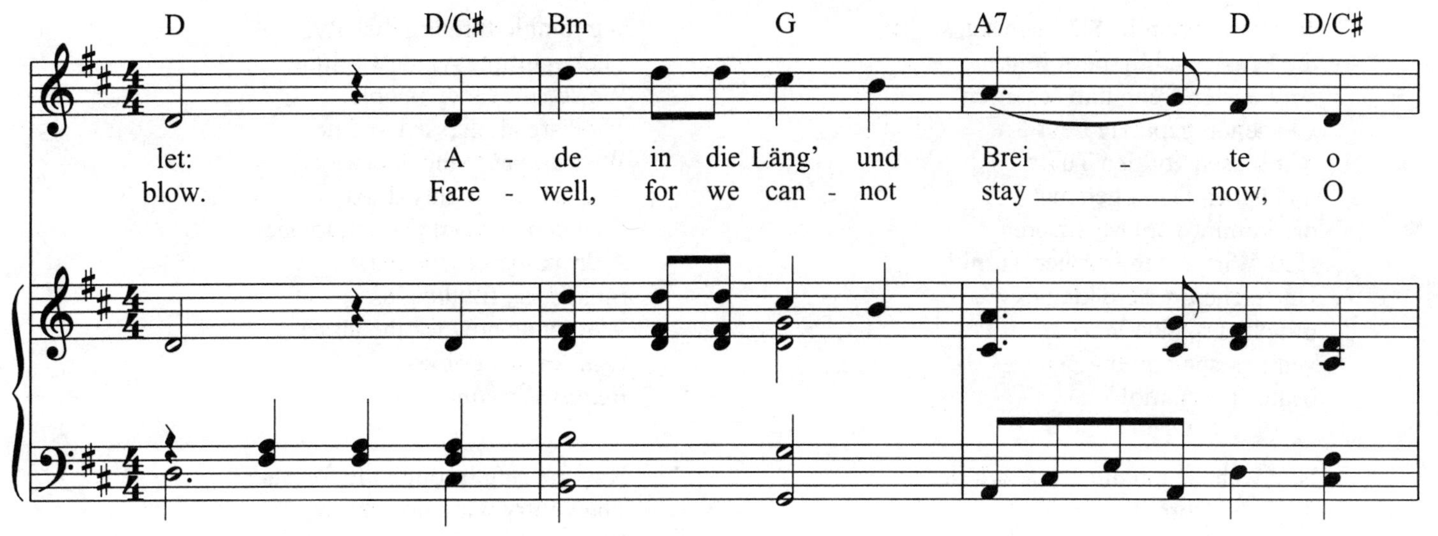
D D/C♯ Bm G A7 D D/C♯
let: A - de in die Läng' und Brei - te o
blow. Fare - well, for we can - not stay now, O

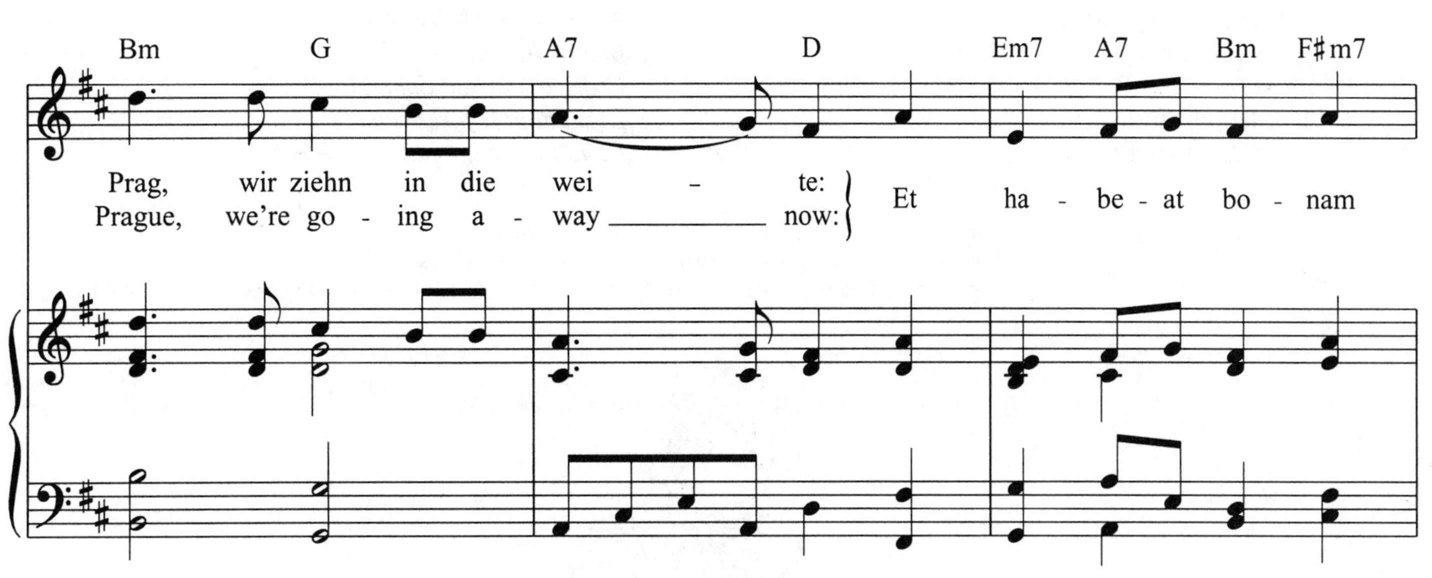
Bm G A7 D Em7 A7 Bm F♯m7
Prag, wir ziehn in die wei - te:
Prague, we're go - ing a - way now:
Et ha - be - at bo - nam

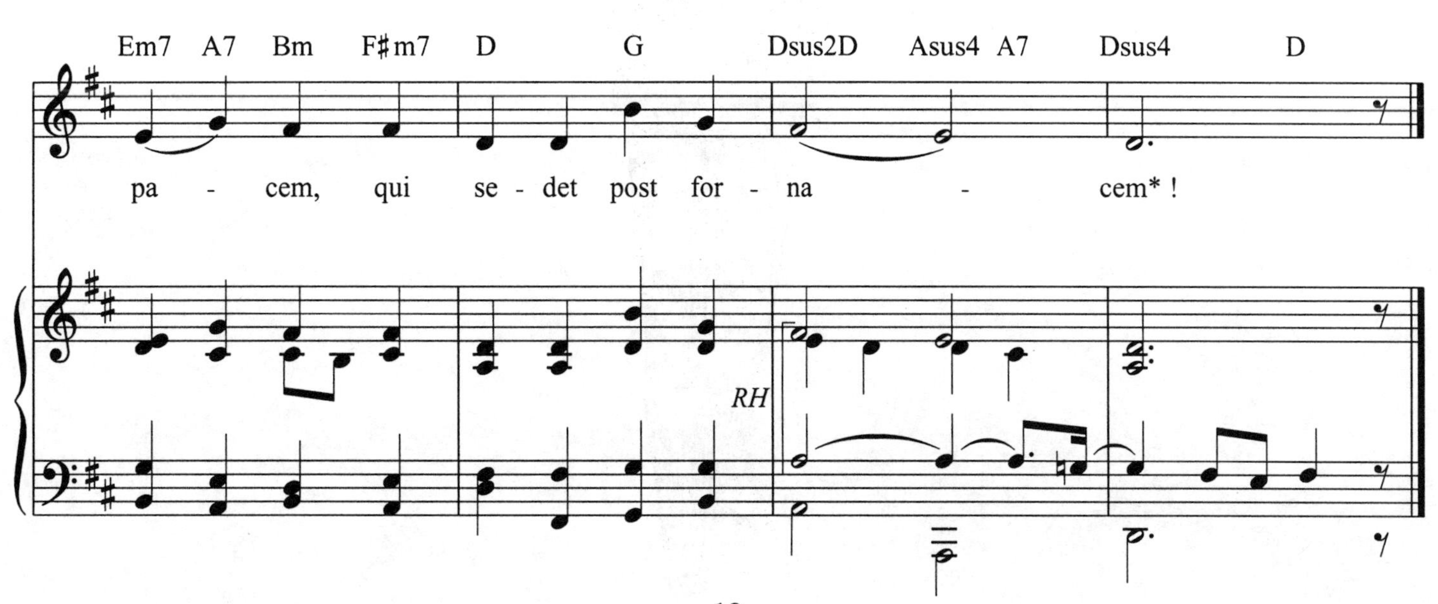
Em7 A7 Bm F♯m7 D G Dsus2D Asus4 A7 Dsus4 D
pa - cem, qui se - det post for - na - cem* !
RH

Nachts wir durchs Städtlein schweifen,
die Fenster schimmern weit,
am Fenster drehn und schleifen
viel schön geputzte Leut'.
Wir blasen vor den Türen
und haben Durst genung,
das kommt vom Musizieren,
Herr Wirt, einen frischen Trunk!
Und siehe über ein kleines
mit einer Kanne Weines
venit ex sua domo -
beatus ille homo!

We ramble through the city,
The nighttime windows shine.
We see the fancy people,
They are all dressed so fine.
We trumpet at the doorways,
And raise a mighty thirst;
That comes from playing music
A drink, before we burst!
Innkeeper, fill the glasses
With wine now for the lasses.
Venit ex sua domo -
Beatus ille homo! * *

Nun weht schon durch die Wälder
der kalte Boreas,
wir streichen durch die Felder,
von Schnee und Regen naß,
der Mantel fliegt im Winde,
zerrissen sind die Schuh',
da blasen wir geschwinde
und singen noch dazu:
Beatus ille homo
qui sedet in sua domo
et sedet post fornacem
et habet bonam pacem!

Now roaring through the forests,
The wintry wind does blow.
We wander over meadows,
All wet with ice and snow.
Our coats flap in the breezes,
And worn out are our shoes.
We blow our horns so gaily,
And sing our halleloos.
Beatus ille homo,
Qui sedet in sua domo,
Et sedet post fornacem,
Et habet bonam pacem! * * *

* He who sits by his stove has good peace.
* * Blessed is the man who comes away from his house.
* * * Blessed is the man who sits in his house and sits by his stove and who has good peace.

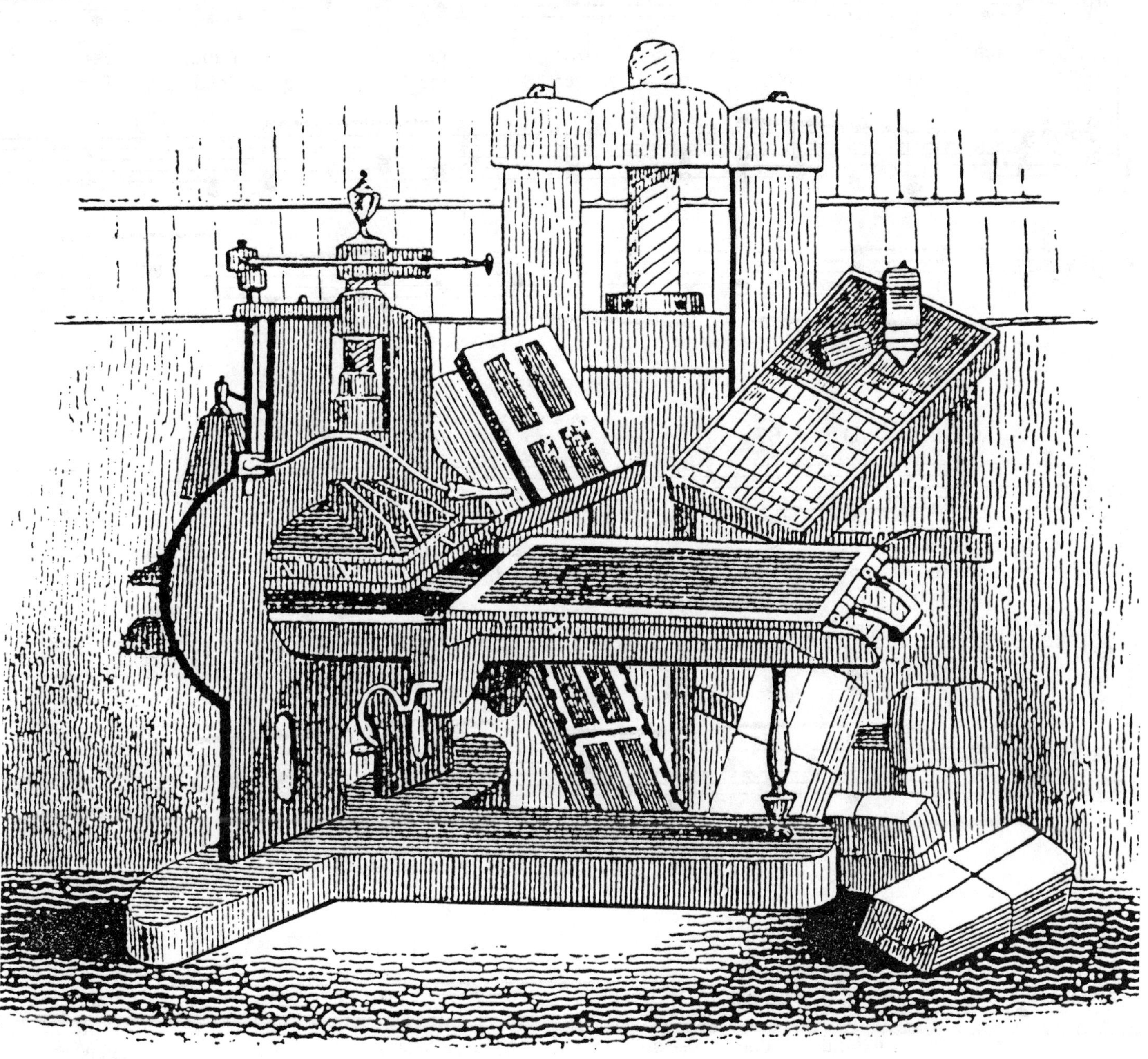

Ich reise übers grüne Land
I Travel Over The Green Land

Words by Joseph von Eichendorff

Music by Hans Engel

A
E7
A
E7
Ich rei - se ü - bers grü - ne Land, der
I tra - vel o - ver the green land, For
A
D
B7
A
E
E7
Win - ter is ver - gan - gen. Hab um den Hals ein
win - ter now is end - ed. A - round my neck, a
A
F♯m
D
B7
E7sus4
E7
A
gül - den Band, dar - an die Lau - te han - gen.
gold - en band, On it my lute's sus - pend - ed.

Der Morgen tut ein' roten Schein,
den recht mein Herze spüret.
Da greif ich in die Saiten ein,
der liebe Gott mich führet.

So silbern geht der Ströme Lauf,
fernüber schallt Geläute,
die Seele ruft in sich: ›› Glück auf! ‹‹
Rings grüßen frohe Leute.

Mein Herz ist recht von Diamant,
ein Blum von Edelsteinen:
die funkelt lustig übers Land
in tausend schönen Scheinen.

Wie bist du schön! Hinaus!
Im Wald gehn Wasser auf und unter;
im grünen Wald sing, daß es schallt:
mein Herz, bleib frei und munter!

The morning has a rosy glow,
My heart, it is affected.
I pluck the strings, both high and low.
By God I am directed.

So silvery the streams do run.
The distant bells are ringing.
My soul cries out, "You lucky one!"
All 'round are people singing.

My heart is like a diamond,
A flower of bright confections,
That sparkles bright o'er all the land,
With myriad reflections.

You are so fair! Begone, begone!
The forest streams are playful.
The forest echoes with my song,
My heart, be free and joyful!

Wohlan die Zeit ist kommen
Indeed, The Time Is Now At Hand

In early springtime, young apprentice boys in pre-industrial associations left their cramped quarters and took to the road. Often, in the course of their vagabondage, they encountered wandering musicians, students, jugglers and all kinds of rovers, whom need had cast upon the road.

C F C Dm7 G7 C F C
Wohl _ an die Zeit ist kom - men, mein Pferd, das muß ge - sat - telt sein, Ich _
In - deed, the time is now at hand, That I must sad - dle up my horse, For _
F C C7 Dm7 G7 C
Chorus
hab mir's vor - ge - nom - men, ge - rit - ten muß es sein.
I my - self have prom - ised, He must go on a course.
Fi - di -
F C G7 C F C
ru - la, ru - la, ru - la-la-la - la - la, fi - di - ru - la, ru - la, ru - la - la.
Ich _
For _
F C C♯dim D7 G7 C
hab mir's vor - ge - nom - men, ge - rit - ten muß es sein.
I my - self have prom - ised, He must go on a course.

Lines 3 and 4 of each verse are sung to the last 4 measures of their respective choruses.

In meines Vaters Garten,
da stehn viel schöne Blum, ja Blum.
Drei Jahr muß ich noch warten,
drei Jahr sind bald herum. *(Chorus)*

Du glaubst, du wärst die Schönste
wohl auf der ganzen Welt, ja Welt,
und auch die Angenehmste,
ist aber weit gefehlt. *(Chorus)*

Der Kaiser streit für's Ländle,
der Herzog für sein Geld, ja Geld,
und ich streit für mein Schätzle,
solang es mir gefällt. *(Chorus)*

Solang ich leb auf Erden,
sollst du mein Trimple Trample sein,
und wenn ich einst gestorben bin,
so trampelst hinterdrein. *(Chorus)*

All in my father's garden,
There are so many pretty flowers.
Three years must I still wait here;
I'm counting all the hours. *(Chorus)*

You think you are the fairest
In every land and every place,
And also the very dearest -
That's really not the case. *(Chorus)*

The kaiser fights for country,
The duke fights for his gold, you see.
And I do fight for my sweetheart,
Just while it pleases me. *(Chorus)*

As long as I am living,
My heart's delight you'll always be;
And when at last one day I die,
You'll follow after me. *(Chorus)*

Reiterabschied
Rider's Farewell

G D7 G C G D7

Wer be - küm - mert sich drum, wenn ich wan - dre bei so schö - ner Som - mers –
Who is griev - ing so be - cause I'm wan - d'ring In this pret - ty sum - mer –

G E7 Am D7

zeit? Ist's die ei - ne nicht, so ist's die an - dre, wer be -
time? If it's not one, then it is the oth - er. Who is

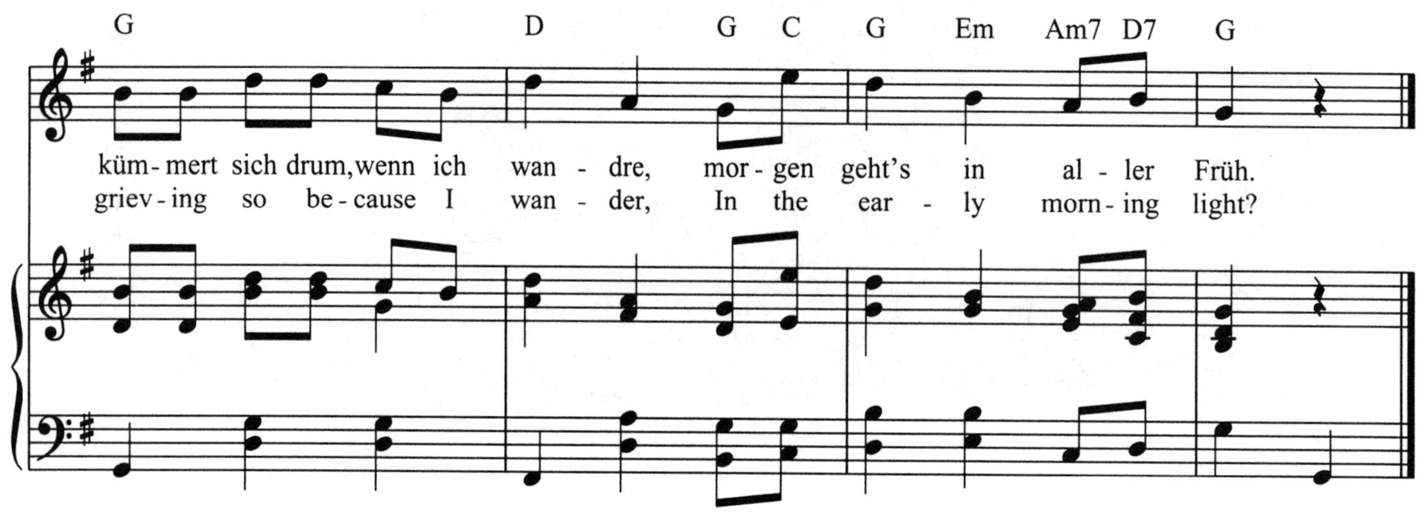
G D G C G Em Am7 D7 G
küm - mert sich drum, wenn ich wan - dre, mor - gen geht's in al - ler Früh.
griev - ing so be - cause I wan - der, In the ear - ly morn - ing light?

Ich habe noch zwei Pistolen,
zu betreiben einen Schuß,
meinem Schätzlein zu gefallen,
sie ist ja die Schönste von allen;
schade, daß ich von ihr muß.

I still have left some money,
I'll spend it quick, you know.
It's all to please my sweetheart,
She's the prettiest of them all.
Too bad I have to go.

Sie dreht sich herum und weinet,
denn der Abschied fällt ihr schwer.
Ihre Äuglein die geben Wasser,
ihre Äuglein die geben Wasser,
fließet in das tiefe Meer.

She wanders around while weeping;
Does not want to part from me.
From her eyes water is flowing,
From her eyes water is flowing,
Flowing to the deep-blue sea.

Die Nacht hat mich überfallen,
ich muß bleiben hier im Wald.
Hier muß ich mein Zelt aufschlagen,
hier muß ich mein Leben wagen,
hier in diesem grünen Wald.

By night I am overtaken,
I must stay here in the woods.
Here, then, must I pitch my tent,
Risk my life and be content,
Here in these green, dismal woods.

Und so geb ich meinem Roß die Sporen.
Zu dem Tor reit ich hinaus.
Schatz, du bleibst mir auserkoren,
Schatz, ach Schatz, du bleibst mir auserkoren,
bis ich wieder komm' nach Haus.

And so I spur my horse ever onward,
To the gate I ride away.
Darling, you remain my chosen,
Oh my dear, you are my chosen,
Until I return some day.

Muß i denn zum Städtele hinaus
Must I Then Leave The City

C G7 C G7 C
Muß i denn, muß i denn zum _ Städ - te-le hin- aus, Städ - te-le hin-aus, und _
komm, wenn i komm, wenn i wie - de-rum _ komm, wie - de-rum _ komm, kehr i
Must I then, must I then leave the cit - y far be-hind, cit - y far be-hind, While _
come, when I come, when I come back once more, come back once more, I will
G7 C G7 C G7
1. 2.
du, mein Schatz, bleibst hier? Wenn i dir. Kann i glei net all - weil
ein, mein Schatz bei
you, my dear, re - main? When I gain. If I can not al - ways
be with you a -
C C7 F C
bei dir sein, han i doch mein Freud an _ dir. Wenn i komm, wenn i komm, wenn i
be with you, still you'll al - ways be my _ joy. When I come, when I come, when I

C A7 Dm7 G7 C
wie - drum_ komm, Wie - drum_ komm, kehr i ein, mein Schatz, bei dir.
come back once more, come back once more, I will be with you a - gain.

Wie du weinst, wie du weinst, daß i wandere muß,
wandere muß,
wie wenn d'Lieb jetzt wär vorbei;
sind au drauß, sind au drauß der Mädele viel,
Mädele viel,
lieber Schatz, i bleib dir treu.
Denk du net, wenn i ein andre seh,
no sei mei Lieb vorbei.
Sind au drauß, sind au drauß der Mädele viel,
Mädele viel,
lieber Schatz, i bleib dir treu.

How you cry, how you cry, that I must travel on,
Must travel on,
As if our love were through.
Even though, even though there are so many girls,
So many girls,
Dearest love, I will be true.
Do not think, do not think when I see another one,
That my love for you is through.
Even though, even though there are so many girls,
So many girls,
Dearest love, I will be true.

Über's Jahr, über's Jahr, wenn mer Träubele schneidt,
Träubele schneidt,
stell i hier mi wiedrum ein;
bin i dann, bin i dann dein Schätzele noch,
Schätzele noch,
so soll die Hochzeit sein.
Über's Jahr, do ist mein Zeit vorbei,
do g'hör i mein und dein.
Bin i dann, bin i dann dein Schätzele noch,
Schätzele noch,
so soll die Hochzeit sein.

In a year, in a year, when the grapes are all picked,
Grapes are all picked,
Then I will return again.
Then I'll be, then I'll be your sweetheart once more,
Sweetheart once more,
Our wedding will take place.
In a year is when my time is up,
The time will then be ours.
Then I'll be, then I'll be your sweetheart once more,
Sweetheart once more,
Our wedding will take place.

Drei Zigeuner
Three Gypsies

Poet Nikolaus Lenau (1802–1850) lived a troubled, wandering life. He was born in Hungary (then part of the Austro-Hungarian Empire), studied philosophy, medicine and law at Vienna and Bratislava, but never entered any profession. He began writing poetry, but under the pressure of censorship he felt compelled to emigrate to America, landing in Baltimore in October 1832. He settled in Ohio, where he remained but one unhappy year, returning to Vienna in October 1833. A continuing, unhappy and impossible love affair literally drove him insane, and he ended his days in an asylum. "Three Gypsies" was published in 1844 in a collection entitled *Waldlieder* ("Forest Songs").

Words by Nikolaus Lenau
Music by Theodor Meyer-Steineg
G D7 G Em Am D7
Drei Zi- geu - ner fand ich ein- mal lie - gen an ei - ner Wei - de,
Once three gyp - sies I chanced to meet, Rest - ing in a pleas- ant mead - ow.
G C G C G D7 G
als mein Fuhr- werk mit mü - der Qual schlich durch die san - di - ge Hei - de.
As my wa - gon did roll through the peat, O - ver the gra - vel - ly trail - o.

Hielt der eine für sich allein
in den Händen die Fiedel,
spielte, umglüht vom Abendschein,] 2
sich ein feuriges Liedel.

Hielt der zweite die Pfeif' im Mund,
blickte nach seinem Rauche,
froh, als ob er vom Erdenrund] 2
nichts zum Glücke mehr brauche.

Und der dritte behaglich schlief,
und sein Cimbal am Baum hing,
über die Saiten der Windhauch lief,] 2
über sein Herzein Traum ging.

Then did gypsy number one,
Hold his fiddle tightly,
Playing, in the setting sun,] 2
A fiery song so brightly.

Number two just smoked on his pipe,
As the smoke was rising;
Needing nothing more in life–] 2
Just that moment prizing.

And the third was fast asleep,
Near by his cembalom hanging.
Over the strings the breezes did creep,] 2
As he was pleasantly dreaming.

An den Kleidern trugen die drei
Löcher und bunte Flicken;
aber sie boten trotzig und frei] 2
Spott den Erdengeschicken.

Dreifach haben sie mir gezeigt,
wenn das Leben uns nachtet,
wie man's verraucht, verschläft und vergeigt,] 2
wie man es dreimal verachtet.

Nach den Zigeunern lang noch schaun
mußt ich im Weiterfahren,
nach den Gesichtern dunkelbraun,] 2
den schwarz lockigen Haaren.

On the clothes that were worn by the three,
Were holes and colorful patches;
But they lived a life that was free,] 2
Scornful of earthly attachments.

Three ways they did show unto me,
When life's shadows lengthen;
Smoke away, sleep away, fiddle away,] 2
Our spirits threefold strengthen.

Long time I gazed after the three,
Oh, I would travel along there,
After the dark-brown faces I see,] 2
And their raven-black long hair.

Das Pfannenflickerlied
The Tinker's Song

The itinerant tinker was a well-known character of somewhat dubious repute throughout Europe. He could repair almost any household item, and often left the grateful housewife longing for a return visit.

E
A
F#7
B7
Und wer das Pfan-nen-flick-en gut ver - steht, der
hat sein täg - lick
lei - det kei - ne
Who - ev - er tin - ker - ing does un - der - stand, he
earns his dai - ly
ne - ver is in

1. E
2. E
A
Brot. Und Not. Der Pfan - nen - flick — er macht sich nicht
bread. Who need, The jol - ly tin — ker, he earns his

E
B7
E
draus, zieht sei - nen Weg von Haus zu Haus.
pay. From house to house he makes his way.

Da kam er am ein großes Tor,
ein Bettler stand davor.
Da kam er an ein schönes Haus,
eine Mamsel schaut heraus.
» Herr Pfannenflicker, kommt doch herein,
hier wird schon was zu flicken sein. «

Da gab sie ihm ein Pfännelein,
das war so schwarz wie Ruß,
darinnen war ein Löchelein,
so groß wie ein Ochsenfuß.
» Herr Pfannenflick, gebt doch in acht,
daß ihr das Loch nicht größer macht.«

Und als das Pfännlein fertig war,
so schön war es geflickt.
Da hat sie ihm ein Dreimark-Stück
in seine Hand gedrückt.
Herr Pfannenflick schwenkt seinen Hut,
» Adjö, Mamsel, die Pfann war gut. «

He came upon a great big door,
A beggar stood before.
He came upon a pretty house,
A lady did look out.
"Oh, Mister Tinker, please do come in,
There's a lot of tinkering to begin."

She gave to him a frying pan,
That was as dark as soot.
And in it was a little hole,
As big as an oxen foot.
"Oh, Mister Tinker, if you will,
Don't make the hole grow bigger still."

And when the pan was all repaired,
The hole was nice and tight.
She pressed on him a three-mark piece,
So new and shiny bright.
He tipped his hat, as well he should,
"Adieu, Ma'm'selle, the pan was good."

Es zogen drei Sänger
Three Singers Did Travel

E A B7 E
1.
Es zo - gen drei Sän - ger wohl ü - ber den Rhein, sie
san - gen ein lu - sti - ges Lie - de-
Three sin - gers did trav - el well o - ver the Rhine. They
lust - i - ly sang out while keep - ing in
2. E A E
lein. Sie san - gen's mit drei - er - lei Stim - men, daß die
time. Their voic - es did blend in a tri - o, And the
A C♯7 F♯m B7 E
Chorus
B7
Ber - ge, daß die Tä - ler er - klin - gen. Tra - la
moun - tains and the val - leys did e - cho.
E A B7 E
la - la - la, tra - la - la, la - la - la - la - la.

Das hörte des Königs Töchterlein
in ihrem stillen Kämmerlein
›› Mit den Sängern da möcht ich wohl reisen,
denn das Singen, das ist meine Freude. ‹‹ *(Chorus)*

Und sie kamen an einen grasgrünen Wald,
da standen die Rosse stille gar bald:
›› Hier im Walde da wollen wir bleiben,
denn die Ross und wir alle seins müde. ‹‹ *(Chorus)*

Und er breitete seinen Mantel aus,
und er setzte vor sich sein Feinsliebchen darauf.
Und er schaute Feinsliebchen ins Angesicht:
›› Feinsliebchen, was bist du so traurig? ‹‹ *(Chorus)*

›› Was sollte ich denn nicht traurig sein,
ich bin ja des Königs Töchterlein.
Und hätt' ich mein's Vaters Rat befolgt,
ein Kaiserkron wär' mir geworden. ‹‹

The king's daughter heard the three travellers sing,
In her chamber she never had heard such a thing.
"I would travel with them at my leisure,
For singing, it is my great pleasure." *(Chorus)*

And soon they arrived at a green grassy wood,
Where quietly waiting, their horses all stood.
"Here in the woods it is best,
For we and the horses need rest." *(Chorus)*

He then spread his coat upon the grass,
And sat on it next to his sweet, loving lass.
He gazed at her so tenderly.
"Dear, why are you sad? Won't you tell me?" *(Chorus)*

"My sadness is a dreadful thing,
I am the daughter of a king;
And had I heeded what he did say,
A royal crown I'd wear today." *(Chorus)*

Hörst du die Landstraß'
Hark To The Highway

C F C A
Hörst du die Land - straß', wie sie lockt und ruft? Schnür dein Bün - del, komm!
Hark to the high - way, cal - ling ev'-ry-where. Tie your bun - dle, come!
Dm D7 G D7 G
Drau - ßen da weht ei - ne an - de - re Luft, drau - ßen scheint die Sonn'. A -
Out - side is blow - ing a breath of fresh air, Out - side shines the sun. Fare -
Am6 B7 Em add f♯ Em6 Dm add e G7 Csus4 2 C
de, mein lie - bes Mä - del, fällt es auch schwer,
well, my dear - est sweet - heart, It is so hard.
Dm7 C Am Fm6 C G7sus4 G7 C
a - ber die Land - straß' läßt uns nim - mer - mehr.
You know the high - way beck - ons us a - far.

Komm, meine Fiedel, wir wandern beide aus
in die weite Welt.
Treibt uns nach Jahren die Sehnsucht nach Haus,
so lang sie uns nicht hält.
Die Landstraß' schon von weitem lockt und ruft,
komme, Geliebter,
hier weht andere Luft.

Mädel in der Heimat, weine nicht so sehr,
weil ich wandern muß.
Die Äuglein so trüb und das Herze so schwer,
Tränen nimmermehr.
Küßt dich auf deinen heißen,
roten Mund
vielleicht zum letzten Mal dein Vagabund.

Come, oh my fiddle, together we will roam,
Roaming far and wide.
Years will pass by, we'll be longing for our home,
But we will not bide.
The highway calls now from the distance,
Love, come with me.
Here the air is free.

Darling back at home, please do not cry so,
For I have to roam.
Your eyes so sad and your heart so low,
Do not weep and moan.
One more kiss I give your
Lips that burn.
Who knows if your vagabond will return?

Straßenräuberlied
Highway Robber's Song

G D7 G
Es gibt doch kein schö - ner Le - ben, in der gan - zen
als das Stra - ßen - räu - ber - le - ben, mor - den um das
There is not a fin - er liv - ing, In this wide world
Than to be a high - way rob - ber, kill - ing so as
D7 G D7
wei - ten Weld In den Wäl - dern um - zu - strei - chen,
lie - be Geld.
I've been told, In the for - ests green to wan - der,
to get gold.
G D7 G
gro - ße Leu - te zu er - rei chen, fehlt es uns an
Fan - cy peo - ple there to plun der. If we lack some

D7
G
D7
G
Geld und Kleid, brin - gen uns die Wan - ders - leut.
cash or a cloak, we just rob the wan - d'ring folk.

Kommt ein Herr daher gegangen,
greifen wir ihn herzhaft an;
kommt ein Jude, der muß hangen,
all sein Geld muß unser sein!
Kommt eine Kutsche oder Wagen,
tun wir sie nicht lange fragen,
hauen, stechen, schießen tot,
ist das nicht ein schön Stück Brot?

If a gentleman comes our way,
We hold him for all he's worth.
If a Jew comes, we must hang him;
All his money fills our purse.
Should a coach or wagon near us,
Ask no questions - how they fear us.
Hacking, stabbing, shooting dead -
What a way to earn our bread!

Sehn wir Galg' und Räder stehen,
bilden wir uns herzhaft ein:
Einmal muß es doch geschehen,
einmal muß gehangen sein.
So steigen wir aus dem Weltgetümmel
auf eine Leiter gegen Himmel,
lassen uns vom Wind schwenken aus und ein,
bis wir abgefaulet sein.

If we see the rack or gallows,
We will face them valiantly.
One day it will surely follow,
We'll hang from the gallows tree.
To the world's noise say goodbye,
On a ladder to the sky,
Swinging there both night and day,
Till at last we rot away.

Laßt den Leib am Galgen hangen,
denn er ist der Vögel Speis'.
Laßt ihn hin und her sich wanken,
bis die Knochen werden weiß.
Laßt ihn liegen in der Erden,
von den Würm' gefressen werden.
Weit schöner ist es in der Luft
als in einer Totengruft.

Leave my body on the gallows,
It will be the birds' delight.
Let it swing from side to side,
Until my bones are bleached snow-white.
Leave it lying in the the ground,
And the worms will gather 'round.
It's far better in the air,
Than lying buried deep down there.

Der Bettelvogt
The Bailiff

From the Middle Ages to the French Revolution, bailiffs functioned in society, performing important public duties. "Waterbailiffs" regulated the use of streams for mills and river traffic. Bailiffs also kept a strict eye out for vagrants and homeless people who camped out at the city gates, as well as other undesirables, such as musicians, jugglers, beggars, prostitutes and discharged soldiers.

D A7
Ich war noch so jung und war ___ doch so arm, kein
When I was so young and was so ve - ry poor, No
D B7 Em D
Geld hatt ich mehr im Beu - tel, daß Gott sich mein er - barm. Da
mon - ey was in my pock - et, God pit - ied me for sure. With
F♯m G A7 D G A7
nahm ich mei - nen Stab und mei - nen Bet - tel - sack und pfiff das Va - ter -
beg - gar's bag and staff I soon was on my way, And piped the "Pa - ter
Bm A7 D Bm7 Em7 A7 Bm D D
1. 2.
un - ser den lie - ben lon - gen Tag, und Tag.
Nos - ter" then, all the live - long day. And day.

Und als ich kam gen Heidelberg hinan,
da packten mich die Bettelvögt von hinten und von vorne an.
Der ein packt mich hinten, der andre packt mich vorn:
›› Ei ihr verdammten Bettelvögt, so laßt mich ungeschor'n ‹‹ (2)

Und als ich kam vor dem Bettelvogt sein Haus,
da schaut der alte Spitzbub zum Fenster grad heraus.
Ich dreh mich hastig um und seh nach seiner Frau:
›› Ei du verdammter Bettelvogt, wie schön ist deine Frau! ‹‹ (2)

Den Bettelvogt erfaßt ein grimmer, grimmer Zorn,
er lässet mich gleich werfen in einen tiefen Turm.
Im tiefen, tiefen Turm bei Wasser und bei Brot:
›› Ei du verdammter Bettelvogt, krieg du die schwere Not! ‹‹ (2)

Und wenn der Bettelvogt gestorben erst ist,
man soll ihn nicht begraben wie einen frommen Christ,
Lebendig ihn begraben bei Wasser und bei Brot,
wie mich der alte Bettelvogt begraben ohne Not. (2)

Ihr Brüder, nun seid lustig, der Bettelvogt ist tot!
Er hänget schon am Galgen, tut keinem von uns Not.
In der vergangnen Nacht, am Dienstag, halber neun,
da hab'n sie ihn gehangen in den Galgen hoch hinein. (2)

Er hätt' die schöne Frau beinahe umgebracht,
weil sie mich armen Schelmen so freundlich angelacht.
In der vergangnen Nacht da schaut er noch heraus,
und heut bin ich bei ihr, bei ihr, bei ihr in seinem Haus. (2)

And when I came to Heidelburg with my pack,
The bailiffs did attack me from the front and back.
One grabbed me from the front, the other from the rear.
"Hey, you God-damn' bailiff, don't cut my hair!" (2)

And when I came up to the bailiff's own house,
Out of the window was looking the old louse.
I quickly turned around, and glancing at his *Frau:*
"Hey, you God-damn' bailiff, she's a pretty one - and how!" (2)

The bailiff became as furious as hell,
And had me thrown right there into a deep dungeon cell.
In the deepest, deepest dungeon, on water and on bread:
"Hey, you God-damn' bailiff, I hope that you drop dead!" (2)

And when one day the bailiff by death will be iced,
He just should not be buried like a godly Christ;
But bury him alive, only with water and with bread.
Just as the bailiff did to me, we'll do to him instead. (2)

Hey, brothers, now be happy, the old bailiff is dead!
He's hanging on the gallows — sleep calmly in your bed.
It was last night, a Tuesday, at half-past nine,
They hung him on the gallows high — now ain't that fine! (2)

He almost had his wife so cruelly put to death,
Because she greeted me, poor rascal, with a friendly laugh.
Last night he was still looking out — that no-good louse,
Today I am with her, with her, with her, right in her house. (2)

Das große Reiselied
The Big-Trip Song

D
Lu - stig, lu - stig, ihr lie - ben Brü - der, nun le - get
Joy - ous, joy - ous, my dear - est broth - ers, Now lay your
B7 Em A7 D Em E7
eu - re Sor - gen nie - der und trinkt da - führ ein gut Glas
wor - ries with the oth - ers, And let's drink a good glass of
A A7 D A7 D
Bier, und trinkt da - führ ein gut Glas Bier.
beer, And let's drink a good glass of beer.

Trinkt auf die G'sundheit aller Brüder,
die heut noch reisen auf und nieder,
die sollen uns're Freunde sein. (2)

Drink to the health of all our brothers,
Traveling so far from all the mothers.
May they all be good friends of ours. (2)

Unser Handwerk ist verdorben,
die besten Brüder sind gestorben,
es lebt ja keiner mehr als ich und du. (2)

Our profession is sorely tried now,
And the best brothers have all died now.
There's no one left but you and me. (2)

Zu Lübeck hab ich's angefangen,
nach Hamburg stand dann mein Verlangen,
das schöne Bremen hab ich auch gesehn. (2)

In Lubeck I was a go-getter,
In Hamburg I hoped things would get better,
Then pretty Bremen I also saw. (2)

Dann geht's nach Braunschweig, Hannover, Minden,
von da woll'n wir nach dem Rhein verschwinden,
wohl nach dem alten, heiligen Köln. (2)

We went to Braunschweig, Hannover, Mindin,
Then to the Rhine our way was wendin'
From there to holy, old Cologne. (2)

Wir wollen auch noch Bonn besuchen,
in Bingen gibt's zum Wein auch Kuchen,
bei Mainz, da fließt der Main in' Rhein. (2)

To Bonn we also paid a vist,
Bingen's wine and cakes - exquisite!
In Mainz, the Main flows to the Rhine. (2)

Zu Mannheim werden wir's Glück probieren,
nach Karlsruh' wird der Weg uns führen,
ach, kämen wir in's Elsaß rein!
In Straßburg gibt es guten Wein!

To Mannheim, let us take a chance there,
Then Karlsruh, we could then advance there.
In Alsace we'd have a good time!
In Strassburg there is the best wine!

In Freiburg geht's nicht lang logieren,
wir wollen in die Schweiz marschieren,
nach Basel, Zürich und bis Bern. (2)

In Freiburg, we'll just spend a day there,
To Switzerland, we are now on our way there,
To Basel, Zurich and to Bern. (2)

Dann wollen wir uns auf's Schifflein setzen
und unser junges Herz ergetzen,
wir fahren den Rhein hinab zur See. (2)

Then in a little boat alighting,
And our youthful hearts delighting,
We sail the Rhine down to the sea. (2)

Schifflein, Schifflein tu umschwenken,
tu uns hin nach Lübeck lenken,
wo es angefangen hat. (2)

Sailboat, sailboat, keep on rocking,
Soon in Lubeck we'll be docking,
Where it all at first began. (2)

Denn wer all das hat gesehen,
kann getrost nach Hause gehen,
und sich nehmen ein junges Weib. (2)

He who's seen so many places,
Knows now home is where his place is,
And can marry a young wife. (2)

Der lockere Vogel
The Enticing Bird

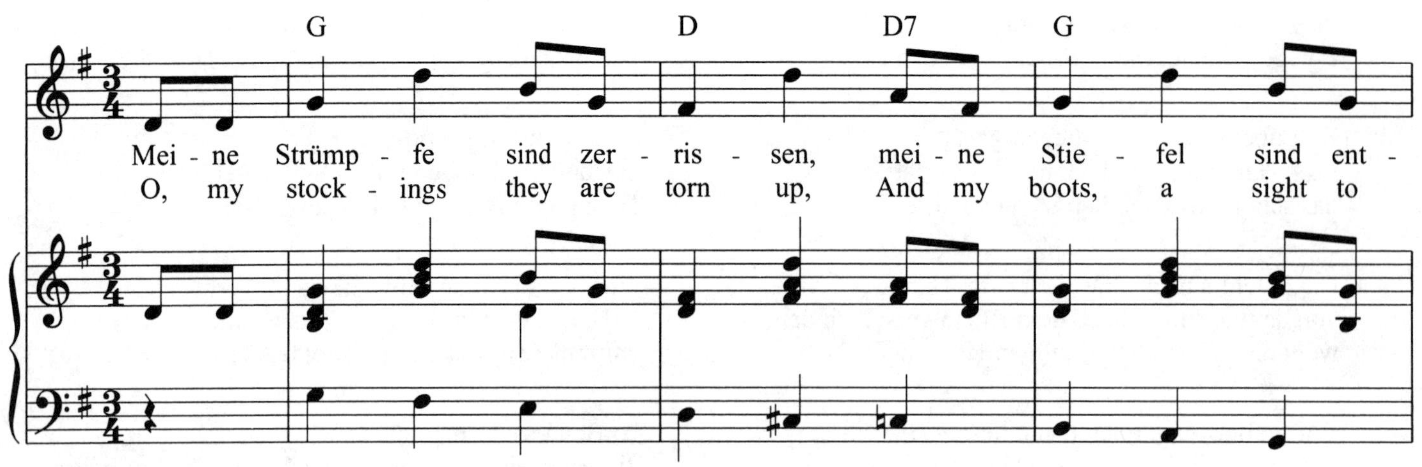
G D D7 G
Mei - ne Strümp - fe sind zer - ris - sen, mei - ne Stie - fel sind ent -
O, my stock - ings they are torn up, And my boots, a sight to

D C G D7 G
zwei, und da drau - ßen auf der Land - straß', da singt der Vo - gel frei.
see, And out - side up - on the high - way, A bird sings bright and free.

Und wär' kein Landstraß' draußen,
da säß ich still zu Haus.
Und wär' kein Loch im Fasse,
so tränk' ich auch nicht draus.

Die Wirtsleut und die Mädel,
die schreien all: ›› O weh! ‹‹
Die Wirtsleut, wenn ich komme,
die Mädel, wenn ich geh'.

And were there no highway outside,
Then at home you'd find me here.
If the barrel had no hole,
Then I would not drink the beer.

The innkeepers and the young girls,
They all cry out, "Oh, no!"
The innkeepers, when I enter,
And the young girls, when I go.

In dem kleinen Oldenburger Land
In The Little Oldenburger Land

D A7
In dem klei - nen Ol - den - bur - ger Land, mit dem Na - tur - stenz in der
In the lit - tle Ol - den - bur - ger land, A hik - ing stick right in their
D G A7 D
Hand, hat sich wie - der ein - ge - fun - den ei - ne Schar von
hand, Once a - gain there did ar - rive there Quite a bunch of
Emsus4 Em D A A7 D
lau - ter duf - ten Kun - den. Und sie tal - fen und sie zot - teln und sie
nois - y, smel - ly guys there. They went beg - ging, they went steal - ing, and they
Em A7 D A7 D
schmie - ren char - mant in dem klei - nen Ol - den - bur - ger Land.
drank so char - mant, In the lit - tle Ol - den - bur - ger land.

Wie jeder Kunde weiß,
ist es im Oldenburg'schen heiß,
denn die Herren vom Teckelgeschlechte
sind fürwahr die reinsten Henkersknechte.
Von oben bis unten wird man bespannt
in dem kleinen Oldenburger Land.

As every wise guy knows,
In Oldenburg, keep on your toes.
For the "gentlemen" policemen,
Are, indeed, the purest hangmen.
They'll string you up at every hand,
In the little Oldenburger land.

Der Herr Amtsanwalt er spricht:
›› Schon wieder ein bekanntes Gesicht.
Das ist sicher einer von den alten
in Lumpen eingewickelten Gestalten.
O welch eine Last für den Beamtenstand
in dem kleinen Oldenburger Land.‹‹

The chief attorney speaks his piece:
"Here comes an old familiar face.
This is one of the old-timers, surely,
In rumpled rags and looking poorly.
It's a load that we can't stand,
In the little Oldenburger land."

Vater Philipp vom Gericht,
er schont die armen Kunden nicht,
er läßt sie wacker klopfen auf die Steine,
daß ihn'n wackeln die Arme und die Beine,
denn so nur vergeht die Lust am Kundenstand
in dem kleinen Oldenburger Land.

The prison warden of the city,
For these bums has little pity.
He has them bravely bang upon the stones,
Till it rattles all their bones.
He works them till they cannot stand,
In the little Oldenburger land.

Wer hat denn dieses Lied er dacht?
Ein dufter Kunde hat's gemacht.
Man nennt ihn den langen Ludwig,
jetzt sitzt er in der Wechte und bessert sich.
Ein Jahr lang ist er auf die Winde verbannt
von dem kleinen Oldenburger Land.

Who has composed this little song?
A stinking wiseguy as he went along.
As "long Ludwig," he is known to all.
Now he's in the pen and he's having a ball.
One year in the workhouse, was the command,
In the little Oldenburger land.

Naturstenz	Naturstock
talfen	betteln
zotteln	stehlen
schmieren	trinken
heiß	sehr gefährlich
Teckelgeschlechte	Gendarmen
bespannt	aufmerksam gemustert
Vater Philipp	Gefängniswärter
Wechte	Landeskorrektionsanstalt in Oldenburg
Winde	Arbeitshaus

Die Wanderschaft
Wandering

C
G7
Die Wan - der- schaft ist schö - ner noch als sit - zen still zu
Now, wan - der- ing is bet - ter yet Than stay - ing in your
C
F
C
Haus. Und pfeift der Wind in Är - mel - loch, er
home. The wind it blows right up your sleeve, It
G7
C Dm7 C
F
pfeift auch wie - der raus. Und pfeift der Wind ins
caus - es you to roam. The wind it blows right
C
G7
C
Är - mel - loch, er pfeift auch wie - der raus.
up your sleeve, It caus - es you to roam.

Wir ziehn zu zwei'n, wir ziehn zu drei'n
durch Sachsenland und Preußen.
Und reißt der Stiefel auch entzwei,] 2
so laß den Schelmen reißen.

›› Frau Wirtin, eine Kanne Wein
für Geld und gute Wort'.
Und kehr ich heut noch bei dir ein,] 2
so muß ich morgen fort.

Und wenn ich morgen weiterzieh',
laß doch das Mahnen sein.
Schreib's nicht an meine Kammertür,] 2
schreib's in den Schornstein rein! ‹‹

We travel by twos, we travel by threes,
Through Saxon land and Prussian.
The boots we wear have holes like cheese,] 2
So let the scoundrels rush on.

"Landlady, please, a jug of wine,
For money and good cheer.
And if I'm here today with you,] 2
By morn I'll disappear.

"Tomorrow, when I'm here no more,
Just leave my bill alone.
Don't write it on my chamber door,] 2
But on your chimney stone."

Als wir jüngst verschütt gegangen waren
Recently We Were Caught In A Round-up

C G C
Als wir jüngst ver - schütt ge - gan - gen wa - ren,
Re - cent - ly we were caught in a round - up,
G7 C
sind wir in dem Grü - nen Au - gust rum - ge - fah - ren
That's when in the Black Ma - ri - a we were bound up:
F C
Mau - er - leu - te, Zim - mer - leu - te und ein Va - ga - bund.
Brick - lay - ers and car - pen - ters, a vag - a - bond, and how!
Am Am7 Dm D7 G7 C
Al - le muß - ten fah - rn in dem Grü - nen Au - gust rund.
Ev' - ry - one must trav - el in the Black Ma - ri - a now.

Und ein Mädchen von siebzehn, achtzehn Jahren
mußte auch mit dem Grünen August fahren.
Weil sie sich herumgetrieben wie ein Fleischerhund,
darum mußr' sie fahren mit dem Grünen August rund.

And a seventeen-or eighteen-year-old girl,
In the Black Maria must go for a whirl.
Like a butcher's dog she acted - she had no pride.
In the Black Maria now she must take a ride.

Und ein Hausierer ohne Papiere
handelt und schachert von Türe zu Türe:
›› Kaufen's Töpfe, Pfannen, Besen, alles billige Sachen! ‹‹
Läuft um die Ecke, dem Teckel in den Rachen.

Then comes a peddler, lacking i. d.
Selling and haggling in doorways goes he.
"Buy my pots and pans and brooms. Prices are low"
Chased by the dogs wherever he does go.

›› Ach Herr Schutzmann, ich hab' doch nichts verbrochen.
Habe nicht gestohlen, und hab' auch nichts gefochten.
Habe nur ein wenig nach der Arbeit ausgeschaut.
Die Ritz -, die Ratz -, die Mausefall', die habe ich verkauft. ‹‹

"Oh, mister watchman, I've broken no laws.
I've stolen nothing, I've given you no cause.
Looking for some work just to make ends meet.
Trying to sell my mousetraps up and down the street."

›› Halt das Maul und laß das Räsonieren!
Rin in den August, da wird dich schon nicht frieren! ‹‹
Zugeklappt und losgefahren, s'ist doch wirklich toll:
Jeden Tag voll Tippelbrüder ist der August voll.

"Shut your mouth and quit your mumbling,
It's hot in the wagon, and away we'll be rumbling!,
Locked inside and rushed away - it is just insane:
Every day the Black Maria is filled up again.

Grüner August	Grüne Minna (Gefangenentransportwagen)
Teckel	Schutzmann (eigentlich Dackel oder Wachhund)

Wandertrost
Wandering's Consolation

C
1. G7
Frisch lu - stig und fröh - lich, ihr Hand - werks _ ge - sel - len, und
tut euch mit ängst - lich - en Sor - gen _ nicht _
Fresh, lust - y and hap - py, you jour - ney - men, _ bless you, And
do not let wor - ri - some trou - bles _ de -
2. G7
Chorus
C F C F F♯dim
quä - len! Denn nicht Reich _ tum macht _ glück - lich: Zu - frie - den - heit macht _
press you! Be - cause rich - es don't make you hap - py; Con - tent - ment will make you
C C7 F C G7 C
reich; wir al - le sind _ Brü - der, wir _ al - le sind gleich.
rich. For we _ are all _ broth - ers, we're _ in the same ditch.

Wir haben schon Kaiser und Könige gesehen, sie tragen goldene Kronen und müssen vergehen; *(Chorus)*	We've already seen kings and kaisers galore. They wear golden crowns, then we see them no more. *(Chorus)*
Der Reiche lebt herrlich in großen Palasten, der Arme der muß ja oft hungern und fasten. *(Chorus)*	The rich man lives grandly in palaces of gold. The poor man must often be hungry and cold. *(Chorus)*

Heut noch sind wir hier zu Haus
Today We're Still At Home

The first verse of this song was already known in 1840. Verses two through five were written by Hoffmann von Fallersleben in 1848. He was a well-known collector of German folk songs.

G Em A7 D D7 G
Heut noch sind wir hier zu Haus, mor - gen geht's zum Tor hin - aus.
While to- day we're still at home, In the morn we're bound to roam.

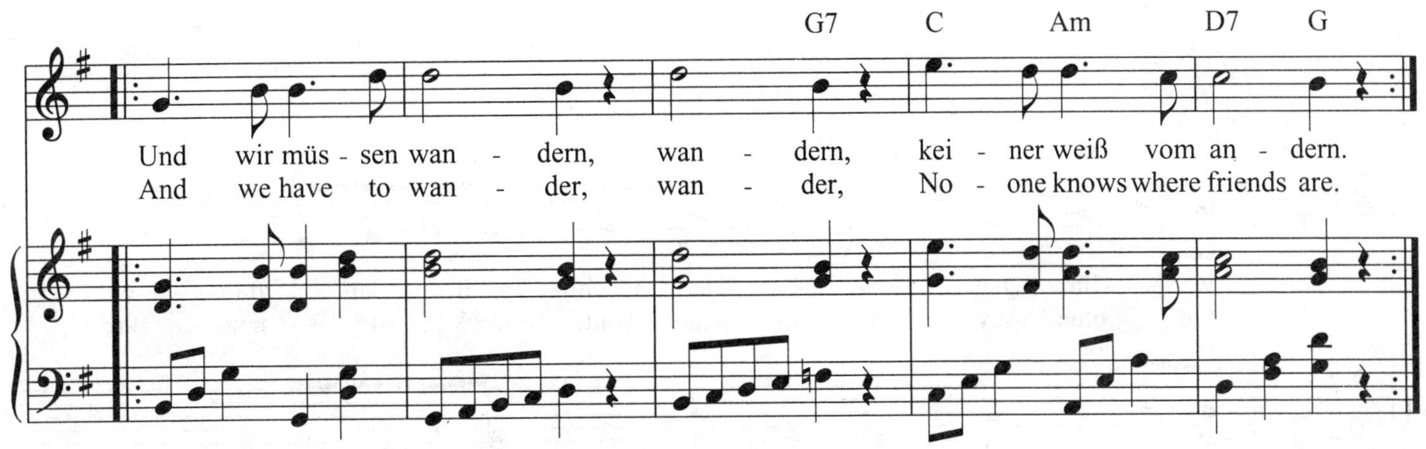

G7 C Am D7 G
Und wir müs - sen wan - dern, wan - dern, kei - ner weiß vom an - dern.
And we have to wan - der, wan - der, No - one knows where friends are.

Lange wandern wir umher
durch die Länder kreuz und quer,
wandern auf und nieder, nieder,] 2
keiner sieht sich wieder.

Long years wandering all around,
Through the country, up and down.
Wandering hither, wandering thither,] 2
No one sees his brother.

Und so wand'r ich immerzu,
fände gerne Rast und Ruh,
muß doch weiter gehen, gehen,] 2
Kält und Hitz' ausstehen.

And I wander ever so.
I would gladly find repose.
I continue touring, touring,] 2
Cold and heat enduring.

Manches Mägdlein lacht mich an,
manches spricht: ›› Bleib, lieber Mann! ‹‹
Ach, ich bliebe gerne, gerne,] 2
muß doch in die Ferne.

Many girls that I do see.
Smile and say, "Please stay with me."
Oh, I would stay gladly, gladly,] 2
But I rush off madly.

Und die Ferne wird mir nah:
Endlich ist die Heimat da!
Aber euch, ihr Brüder, Brüder,] 2
seh' ich niemals wieder.

In the distance, coming near,
Finally my homeland here!
Ah, but you, my brother, brother,] 2
We have lost each other.

Zug der Schwäne
Flight of the Swans

Author Eberhard Koebel spent a year in Lapland. This song reflects his feelings for the northland. The melody is based on a Russian folk tune.

Words by Eberhard Koebel

G Am A7 D D7 G
Ü - ber mein - er Hei - mat Früh - ling seh ich Schwä - ne
O - ver my home white swans do fly, Spring - time, north - ward

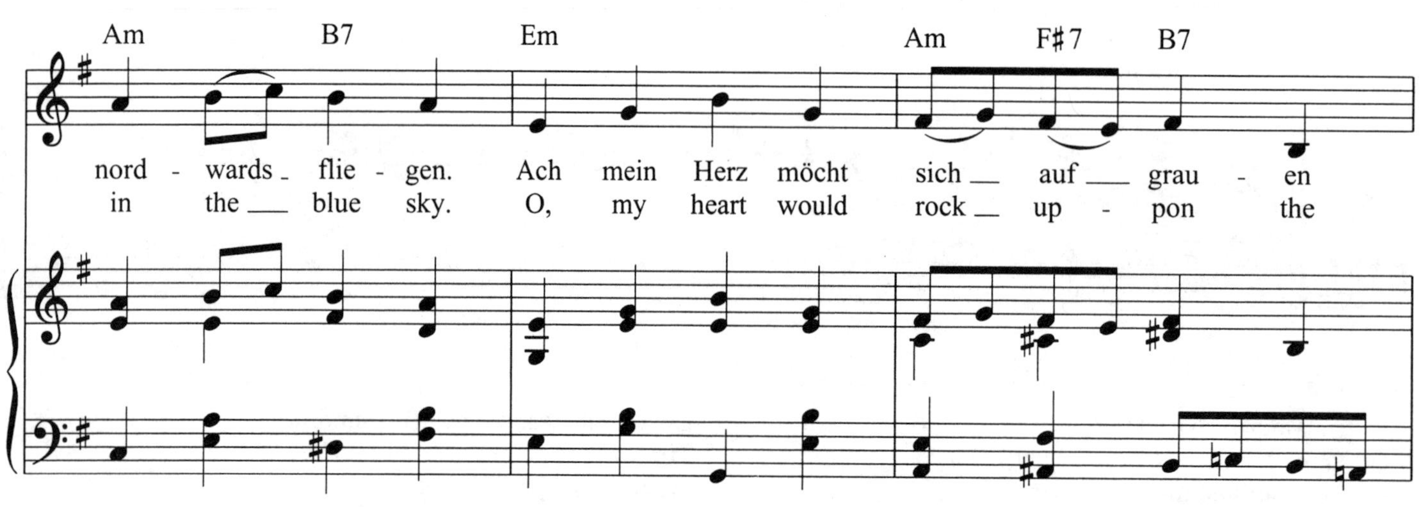
Am B7 Em Am F#7 B7
nord - wards flie - gen. Ach mein Herz möcht sich auf grau - en
in the blue sky. O, my heart would rock up - pon the

Em B7 Em
Eis - meer wo - gen wie - gen.
Arc - tic waves so glad - ly.

Schwan im Singsang deiner Lieder
grüß die grünen Birkenhaine.
Alle Rosen gäb ich gerne
gegen Nordlands Steine.

Swan, the message of your singing,
Greets the birch groves, sets them ringing.
All the roses I would exchange,
For the northern mountain range.

Grüß mir Schweden, weißer Vogel,
setz an meiner Statt die Füße
auf den kalten Stein der Ostsee.
Sag ihr meine Grüße.

Say hello to Sweden for me.
Set your feet down on my city.
Greet the rocky Baltic coast,
It's the place I love the most.

Grüß das Eismeer, grüß das Nordkap,
ruf den Schären zu, den Fjorden,
wie ein Schwan sei meine Seele
auf dem Weg nach Norden.

Greet the Arctic, greet the North Cape,
Hail the flocks and hail the fjords.
Let my soul be like a swan,
As it voyages northwards.

Auf, du junger Wandersman
Up, You Youthful Wandering One

G Am A7 D
Auf, du jun - ger Wan - ders - mann! Jet - zo kommt die Zeit her - an, die
Up, you youth - ful wan - d'ring one! Now the time is com - ing on; The
G Am7 D7 G Dm6 E7 Amsus4 Am7
Wan - der - zeit, die gibt uns Freud. Woll'n uns auf die Fahrt be - ge - ben,
wan - d'ring days that we do praise. We are set to leave to - day now,
D D7 E+7 Amsus4 Am B7 Em Em/D♯ Em/D Em/C♯
das ist un - ser schön - stes Le - ben, gro - ße Was - ser
This is life! That's what I say now. Migh - ty riv - ers,
D D7 G D♯dim Em G Am7 D7 G
Berg und Tal, an - zu - schau - en ü - ber all.
hill and vale, Just to see it with - out fail.

An dem schönen Donaufluß
findet man ja seine Lust
und seine Freud'
auf grüner Heid',
wo die Vöglein lieblich singen
und die Hirschlein fröhlich springen;
dann kommt man vor eine Stadt,
wo man gute Arbeit hat.

Mancher hinter'm Ofen sitzt
und gar fein die Ohren spitzt,
kein Stund vor's Haus
ist kommen raus.
Den soll man als G'sell erkennen
oder gar ein' Meister nennen,
der noch nirgends ist gewest,
nur gesessen in sein'm Nest?

Mancher hat auf seiner Reis'
ausgestanden Müh und Schweiß
und Not und Pein;
das muß so sein.
Trägt's Felleisen auf dem Rücken,
trägt es über tausend Brücken,
bis er kommt nach Innsbruck' rein,
wo man trinkt Tirolerwein!

Morgens, wenn der Tag angeht
und die Sonn' am Himmel steht
so herrlich rot
wie Milch und Blut.
Auf, ihr Brüder, laßt uns reisen,
unserm Herrgott Dank erweisen
für die fröhlich' Wanderzeit,
hier und in die Ewigkeit!

On the pretty Danube stream,
It is there we find our dream.
Joy is ours
'Midst the flowers,
Where the birds are gaily singing,
And the little deer are springing.
Then we come upon a town,
Where a good job can be found.

Many sit at home all day,
Sharpening needles, so they say.
They stay at home,
Never to roam.
Better be a journeyman,
Or a master, if you can.
Who would always be at rest,
At home, sitting in his nest?

In their travels many get
Nothing but fatigue and sweat,
And misery.
So must it be.
With his knapsack's heavy load,
Over bridges - down the road,
Till he comes to Innsbruck town,
Where Tyrol wine is drunk down.

Morning, when the day does break,
And the sun is wide awake,
So wondrous red,
Like milk and blood,
Rise, oh brothers, time to be going,
And to God our thanks be showing.
Wandering now so joyously.
Now and for eternity.

Wenn die Arbeitszeit zu Ende
When The Working Time Is Over

Words by Jürgen Brand

D A E7
Wenn die Ar - beits - zeit zu En - de, rü - sten wir nach Bur - schen -
When the work - ing time is o - ver, we pre - pare for hap - py
A D A E7
art. Sam - stag al - le fleiß' - gen Hän - de zu der fro - hen Wan - der-
days. Sat - ur - day, the eag - er peo - ple set out on their wan - d'ring
A Em E7 A E7 A
fahrt. Sin - gend ziehn wir aus dem Städt - chen,
ways. Sing - ing we do leave the cit - y,
G D Em D A Bm6 A
frei daz Herz und leicht der Zinn.
Spir - its light and heart so free.
Chorus
D
Links die Bur - schen,
Left, the boys and

Em E7 A

rechts die Mäd-chen,und ich sel - ber mit - ten - drin.
right, the girls, And in the mid - dle there is me.

D A7 D

Links die Bur - schen, rechts die Mäd - chen und ich sel - ber mit - ten drin.
Left, the boys and right, the girls, And in the mid - dle there is me.

Hei, das ist ein fröhlich Wandern!
Wiesen, Felder ziehn vorbei.
Einer sagt es froh dem andern:
›› Heute, Bruder, sind wir frei! ‹‹
Weit zurück liegt schon das Städtchen,
und wir wandern leicht dahin. *(Chorus)*

Singen, Spielen im Vereine,
Rast in kühler Waldesruh,
und beim hellen Mondenscheine
wandern wir der Heimat zu.
Singend ziehn wir ein ins Städtchen,
frei das Herz und leicht der Sinn. *(Chorus)*

Hey, this is a happy journey!
Meadows, green fields do we see.
One says gaily to another,
"Brother, today we are free!"
Far behind us lies the city.
We roam happy as can be. *(Chorus)*

Singing, playing with our companions,
In the forest we lie down.
Then in the bright shining moonlight,
We return to our town.
Singing, we enter the city
Spirits light and hearts so free. *(Chorus)*

Ich bin auch in Ravenna gewesen
I Also Paid Ravenna A Visit

Words by Herman Hesse

Music: Traditional

E B7 E C♯m F♯m7 B7
Ich bin auch in Ra - ven - na ge - we - sen, ist ei - ne klei - ne, to - te
I al - so paid Ra - ven - na a vis - it, It is a small and dead old
E A Am E
Stadt, die Kir - chen und viel Ru - i - nen hat, man
town. some church - es and ru - ins you'll see there, In
B7 G♯7 C♯m E7 A Am
kann da - von in Bü - chern le - sen. Die Kir - chen und viel Ru -
books you can read all a - bout them, Some church - es and ru - ins
E G♯7 C♯m F♯7 B7 E
i - nen hat, man kann da - von in Bü - chern le - sen.
you'll see there, In books you can read all a - bout them.

Du gehst hindurch und schaust dich um,
die Straßen sind so trüb und naß,
und sind so tausendjährig stumm,
und überall wächst Moos und Gras.] 2

Das ist, wie alte Lieder sind:
Man hört sie an, und keiner lacht,
und jeder lauscht und jeder sinnt
hernach daran bis in die Nacht.] 2

You walk about and look around,
The streets are wet as you do pass.
In a thousand years they haven't made a sound,
And everywhere grows moss and grass.] 2

It's just like with the old, old songs -
You hear them through, they've lost their bite.
Each person listens and reflects
From now until so late at night.] 2

Der Zugvogel
The Bird Of Passage

A♯dim G7 C C7 F G7 C
Mach mir kein bit - te - res Ge - sicht, es geht nicht, lie - ber Schatz.
Please don't make me a mourn-ful face, It won't work, o, my dear.
C♯dim G7 C E7 Am E7 Am
Was mir dein Herr Pa - pa ver - spricht ist al - les für die Katz'. Denn
Your fath - er's prom-is - es to me Are just words in the air. A
G7 C D7 G G7
Kin - der - wie - gen mag ich nicht und Schrei - ber wer - den beim Ge - richt: Nicht
ba - by cra - dle's not for me, Our wed - ding banns won't post - ed be, All
C F C F C G7 C
um den Rat - haus - platz, nicht um den Rat - haus Platz.
in the court - house square, All in the court - house square.

Die blaue Ferne lockt so sehr,
blaßblau, wie dein korsett.
Ach, wenn ich Berge, Welt und Meer
doch nicht genossen hätt'!
Und wenn Paris Paris nicht wär',
dächt ich vielleicht an Wiederkehr
in dein honettes Bett. (2)

The blue horizon calls to me,
Pale blue like your corset.
Oh, thinking of hills, lands and sea,
That I have not seen yet!
If only Paris were not there,
Then maybe one day I'd repair
Into your honest bed. (2)

Die Pappel dort an der Chaussee
biegt schon der Märzenwind.
Mein Wintertraum zergeht wie Schnee,
der von den Dächern rinnt.
Zu eng wird mir das Nest. Ade!
Familienglück, Kamillentee!
- Und denk an mich, mein Kind! (2)

The poplar there along the road,
The March wind shakes its leaves.
My winter dream does melt like snow
That's dripping from the eaves.
The nest has grown too tight for me,
With family joys, camomile tea!
Think of me and don't grieve. (2)

Das Lieben bringt groß Freud
Loving Brings Great Joy

E A E B7
Das Lie - ben bringt groß'_ Freud', es __ wis - sin's al - le __
Now, lov - ing brings great _ joy, To __ ev' - ry girl and _
E C♯7 F♯m sus4 F♯m B7
Leut'. Weiß _ mir ein schö - nes __ Schät - ze - lein mit __
boy. Show _ me a pret - ty __ lit - tle maid, Two _
E C♯m7 F♯7 B7 E A
zwei schwartz - brau _ nen _ Äu - ge - lein die __ mir, die __
twink - ling eyes _ of __ dark _ brown _ shade, Who _ gives, who _
E B7 E
mir, die __ mir mein Herz er - freut.
gives, Who _ gives my heart great _ joy.

Ein Brieflein schrieb sie mir,
ich soll treu bleiben ihr.
Drauf schickt ich ihr ein Sträußelein,
schön Rosmarin, brauns Nägelein,
sie sollt, sie sollt,
sie sollt mein eigen sein!

Mein eigen sollt sie sein,
kein'm andern mehr als mein.
So leben wir in Freud' und Leid,
bis uns Gott der Herr auseinander scheid't.
Ade, ade,
ade, mein Schatz, ade!

She wrote a *billet doux,*
And hoped that I'd be true.
An ostrich chick to her I sent;
Sweet rosemary, cloves for their scent,
So she'd be mine.
And that is what it meant.

My true love she should be.
No other love than me.
And so for better or for worse,
We live till life has run its course.
Farewell, farewell,
Farewell, my love, farewell.

Wach auf, meins Herzens Schöne
Wake Up, My Dear One

Songs in which the singer bids farewell to his love at daybreak were standard fare in Middle High German poetry. Here we have an authentic example of such a song, dating from around 1547, which has been preserved to the present day (albeit in somewhat altered form).

C G7 C F G7 C
Wach' auf, meins Her - zens Schö - ne, Herz - al - ler - lieb - ste mein! Ich
Wake up, wake up, my dear one, Be - lov - ed, hear my words. I
G7 C C7 F G7 C
hör' ein süß' Ge - tö - ne von klei - ne Wald-vög - lein, die hör' ich so lieb - lich
hear a sound, a clear one, From lit - tle for - est birds, I hear them so sweet- ly
F C Dm6 E7 Am G7 C Dm G7 C
sin - gen, ich mein', ich säh' des Ta - ges Schein vom O - ri - ent her - drin - gen.
sing - ing, I mean, I see the light of day, The east - ern sky is bring - ing.

Ich hör' die Hahnen krähen
und spür' den Tag dabei,
die kühlen Winde wehen,
die Sternlein leuchten frei;
singt uns Frau Nachtigalle,
singt uns ein süße Melodei,
sie neut den Tag mit Schalle.

Selig sind Tag und Stunde
darin du bist gebor'n.
Gott grüß mir dein' rot' Munde,
den ich hab' auserkor'n.
Kann mir kein Lieb're werden,
schau, daß mein Lieb' nit sei verlor'n,
du bist mein Trost auf Erden.

Der Himmel tut sich färben
aus weißer Farb' in blau,
die Wolken tun sich färben
aus schwarzer Farb' in grau,
die Morgenröt' tut herschleichen,
wach auf, mein Lieb', und mach mich frei,
die Nacht will uns entweichen.

I hear the roosters crowing,
And with them comes the day.
The cool winds are a-blowing,
The stars soon fade away.
The nightingale sings for us,
Sings us a charming melody.
The day breaks to its chorus.

Happy the day and hour,
My dear, when you were born.
I thank God for your red lips,
Which I kiss night and morn.
There can be no one dearer.
Know that my love will never falter;
No one on earth is nearer.

The sky is changing color
From white to blue - it's day.
The clouds are changing color
From midnight black to gray.
The morning's red is creeping,
Awake, my love, and set me free;
It's time to end your sleeping.

Es waren zwei Königskinder
There Were Two Royal Children

G D7 G D7 G
Es wa - ren zwei Kö - nigs - kin - der, die hat - ten ein - an - der so
There were two _ ro - yal chil - dren, Their love's tale could make _ you _
D7 G D7 G D7
lieb; sie konn - ten zu - sam - men nicht kom - men, _ das _
weep. They could nev - er come _ to each oth - er, _ The _
G D7 Em D7 G D7 G
Was - ser war viel zu tief, das Was - ser war viel _ zu tief.
wa - ter was much too deep, The wa - ter was much too deep.

›› Ach Liebster, kannst du nicht schwimmen,
so schwimm doch herüber zu mir!
Drei Kerzen will ich anzünden,
und die sollen leuchten dir. ‹‹ (2)

"Oh, dearest, are you a swimmer?
If so, swim over to me!
And then I will light three candles;
You will be able to see." (2)

Das hört eine falsche Nonne,
die tat, als ob sie schlief.
Sie tät die Kerzen auslöschen,
der Jüng ertrank so tief. (2)

A false nun overheard them.
While they were all asleep,
She blew out the three candles.
The youth drowned in the deep. (2)

Es war an ein'm Sonntagmorgen,
die Leute war'n alle so froh,
nicht so die Königstochter,
die Augen saßen ihr zu. (2)

It was on a Sunday morning,
The people were all so gay.
Not so, the king's own daughter,
Her eyes gave her away. (2)

›› Ach Fischer, liebster Fischer,
willst du dir verdienen groß' Lohn,
so wirf dein Netz ins Wasser
und fisch' mir den Königssohn. ‹‹ (2)

"Oh, fisherman, dear fisher,
Do you want a reward?
Cast your net in the ocean,
And haul the prince on board." (2)

Er warf das Netz ins Wasser,
es ging bis auf den Grund;
der erste Fisch, den er fischet,
das war des Königs Sohn. (2)

He cast his net in the water,
It sank down to the ground.
The first fish that he caught there
Was the king's son who had drowned. (2)

Sie faßt ihn in ihre Arme
und küßt seinen toten Mund:
›› Ach Mündlein, könntest du sprechen,
so wär mein jung' Herz gesund! ‹‹ (2)

Into her arms she took him,
Kissed him and then implored,
"Oh, dear mouth could you speak now,
My young heart would be cured." (2)

Was nahm sie von ihrem Haupte?
Eine goldene Königskron:
›› Sieh da, wohledler Fischer,
hast dein' verdienten Lohn! ‹‹ (2)

From off her head she took then
Her royal crown of gold.
"For you, honorable fisherman.
It is as you were told." (2)

Sie schloß ihn an ihr Herze
und sprang mit ihm in die See:
›› Gut Nacht, mein Vater und Mutter,
ihr seht mich nimmermeh! ‹‹ (2)

She clasped him to her bosom,
And leaped with him into the sea.
"Good night, my father and mother,
You'll never more see me." (2)

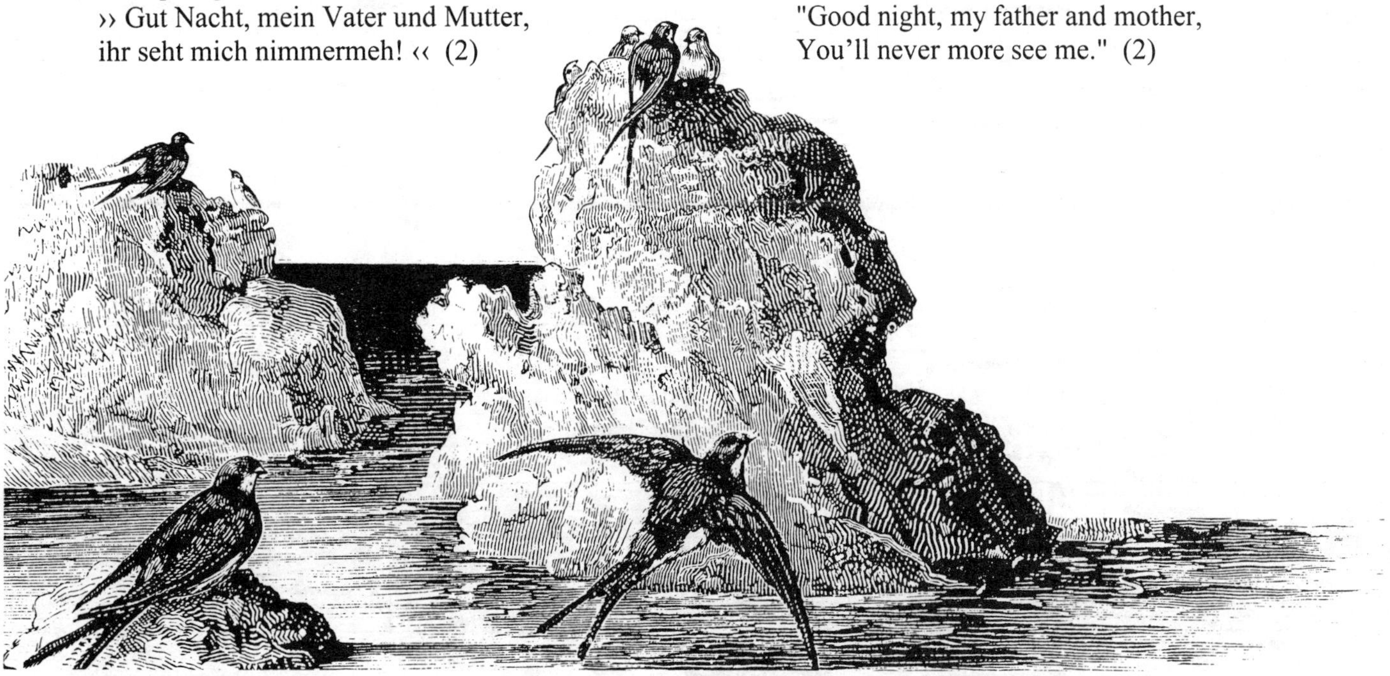

Das zerbrochene Ringlein
The Little Broken Ring

Joseph von Eichendorff studied in Heidelberg. Along the banks of the nearby Rohrbach is a narrow valley, "Im kühlen Grunde," mentioned in the opening of this song.

Words by Joseph von Eichendorff
Music by Friedrich Glück
G D7 Em A7
In ei - nem küh - len Grun - de, da geht ein Müh - len -
In the cool riv - er shal - lows, An old mill wheel goes
D D7 G C
rad, mein Lieb - ste ist ver - schwun - den, die
'round. My true love used to live there, But
G D7 G D7
dort ge - woh - net hat, mein Lieb ste ist ver -
now she can't be found. My true love used to
G7 C G D7 G
schwun - den die dort ge - woh - net hat.
live there, But now she can't be found.

Sie hat mir Treu versprochen,
gab mir ein'n Ring dabei,
sie hat die Treu gebrochen,
mein Ringlein sprang entzwei.]2

Ich möcht als Spielmann reisen
weit in die Welt hinaus
und singen meine Weisen
und gehn von Haus zu Haus.]2

Ich möcht als Reiter fliegen
wohl in die blut'ge Schlacht,
um stille Feuer liegen
im Feld bei dunkler Nacht.]2

Hör ich das Mühlrad gehen:
ich weiß nicht, was ich will -
ich möcht am liebsten sterben,
dann wär's auf einmal still.]2

She gave to me her promise,
A ring to prove her true.
Her promise she did break then,
The ring, it broke in two.]2

I would as a musician,
This wide world travel o'er,
And sing of my condition,
Going from door to door.]2

I would ride off on horseback,
To fight the bloody fight,
And lie next to the campfire
In fields by dark of night.]2

I hear the mill-wheel turning,
I don't know what I will.
I would die for my true love,
It would at once be still.]2

Was hab ich denn meinem Feinsliebchen getan
What Have I Done To My Love

D A7 D
Was hab' ich denn mei - nem Feins - lieb - chen ge - tan? Sie
What have I done to my love? It's a mys - te - ry. She
A A7 D
geht ja vor - ü - ber und schaut mich nicht an. Sie
goes ev - 'ry - where but she does - n't look at me. She
A E7 A A7
schlägt ih - re Äug - lein wohl un - ter sich und
casts her eyes down most all of the time, And
D G D A7 D
hat ei - nen an - de - ren viel lie - ber noch als mich.
val - ues an - oth - er's love much more than she does mine.

Das machet ihr stolzer, hochmütiger Sinn,
daß ich ihr nicht schön und nicht reich genug bin;
und bin ich auch nicht reich, so bin ich doch so jung;
herzallerliebstes Schätzelein, was kümmer' ich mich drum!

Die tiefen, tiefen Wasser, die haben keinen Grund;
laß ab von der Liebe, sie ist dir nicht gesund!
Die hohen, hohen Berge, das tiefe, tiefe Tal,
jetzt seh' ich mein Schätzele zum allerletzten Mal.

It comes from her proud and arrogant schemes,
That I'm not as handsome or as rich as her dreams.
I may not be so rich, but my young heart's on my sleeve.
Oh, dearest sweetheart, it causes me to grieve.

The deepest, deepest water, 'way down beneath the blue;
Give up on this loving, it is not good for you.
The highest, highest mountain, the valley down below;
And now, my dearest sweetheart, from you I'm bound to go.

Es geht eine dunkle Wolk herein
A Dark Black Cloud Is Blowing In

Dm Gm Dm A7 Dm
Es geht ein dunk - le Wolk her - ein, mich deucht, es
A dark black cloud is blow - ing in, I think the
Gm Dm E7 Am E7 Am
wird ein Re - gen sein, ein Re - gen aus den
rain will soon be - gin! A rain come down from
F Dm Gm A7 Dm
Wol - ken wohl in das grü - ne Gras.
heav - en, Down on the dark green grass.

Und kommst du, liebe Sonn', nit bald,
so weset alls im grünen Wald,
und all die müden Blumen,
die haben müden Tod.

Es geht eine dunkle Wolk' herein,
es soll und muß geschieden sein.
Ade, Feinslieb, dein Scheiden
macht mir das Herze schwer.

And if the sun does not return,
The forest creatures all will yearn,
And all the tired flowers
Will die a tired death.

A dark black cloud above I see,
And that's the way it has to be.
Farewell, my dear, your parting,
If weighs upon my heart.

O käm das Morgenrot
Oh, Would The Morning Light

This song arrived in East Prussia from Lithuania.

Em
Am
Em
G
D7
O käm das Mor - gen - rot her - auf,
o ging' die Son - ne doch schon auf!
Oh, would the morn - ing light draw near,
And would the sun - rise soon ap - pear.
Säh' ich her -
Then I'd see

G
C
G
D7
G
D7
G
rei - ten mei - nen Ge - lieb - ten ü - bers Feld.
rid - ing my, dear sweet - heart, O - ver the field.

Und als ich's wünschte, war er da,
rief, als er kam dem Tore nah:
›› Öffne, mein Mädchen, öffne geschwind
und laß' mich ein! ‹‹

›› Warte nur, wart' ein Stündchen noch ‹‹,
sagte ich scherzend. ›› Warte doch!
Wart', lieber Bursche, wart', bis zuletzt
ich Zeit für dich hab'. ‹‹

›› Hast du nicht Zeit für mich, mein Kind?
Und ich ritt her in Nacht und Wind. ‹‹
Er sprach es traurig, wandte sein Roß
und ritt davon.

O käm' das Morgenrot herauf,
o ging'die Sonne doch schon auf!
Säh' ich herreiten meinen Geliebten
übers Feld!

While I was wishing he were here,
He called, and I knew he was near.
"Open, my sweetheart, quick, open the gate,
And let me in."

"Wait, just wait an hour or more,"
Said I, joking, through the door
"Wait, my dear lover, wait just until
I have time for you."

"Have you no time for me, my dear?
All night I've ridden to come here."
He spoke sadly, turned his horse 'round,
And rode away.

Oh, would the morning light draw near,
And would the sunrise soon appear!
Then I'd see riding, my sweetheart,
Over the field.

Die Gedanken sind frei
Our Thoughts Are Ever Free

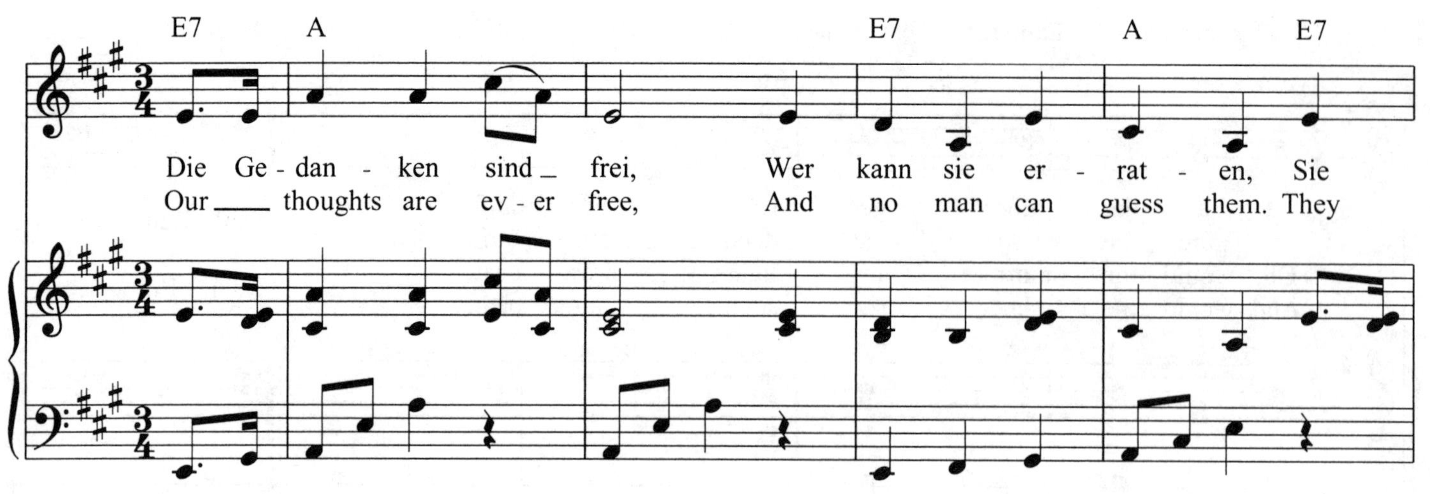
E7 A E7 A E7
Die Ge - dan - ken sind frei, Wer kann sie er - rat - en, Sie
Our thoughts are ev - er free, And no man can guess them. They

A E7 A
flie - hen vor bei, Wie nächt - li - che schat - ten, Kein
fly free from me, As I do ex - press them. No

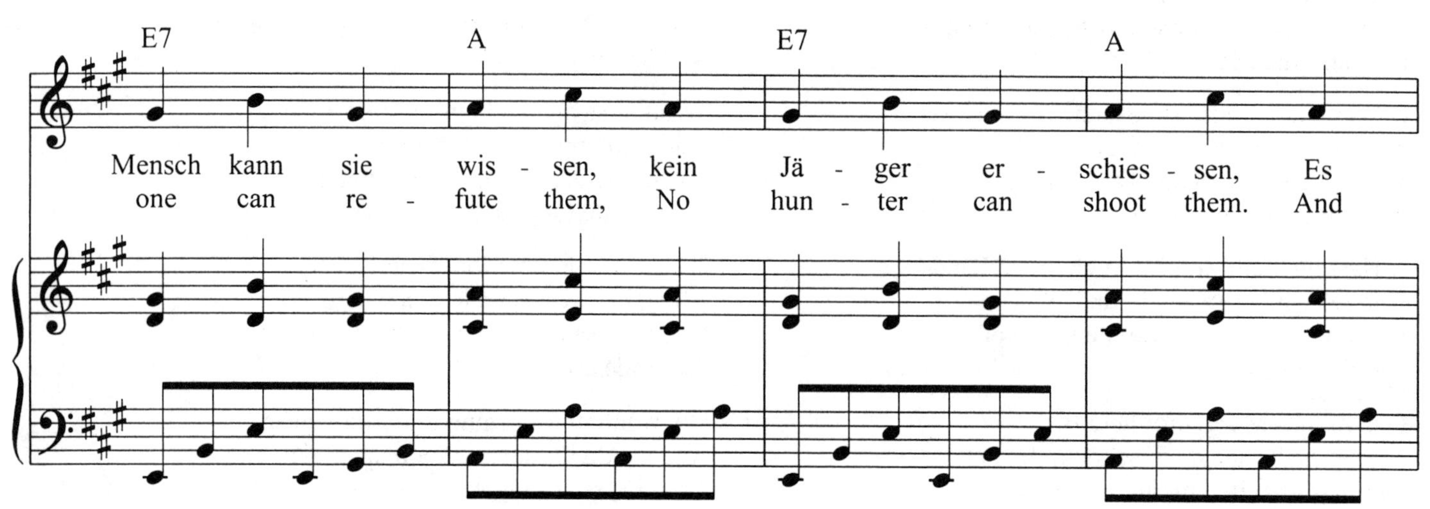
E7 A E7 A
Mensch kann sie wis - sen, kein Jä - ger er - schies - sen, Es
one can re - fute them, No hun - ter can shoot them. And

D
A
E7
A
blei - bet da bei, Die Ge - dan - ken sind frei. Es
so it must be: Our thoughts are ev - er free. And

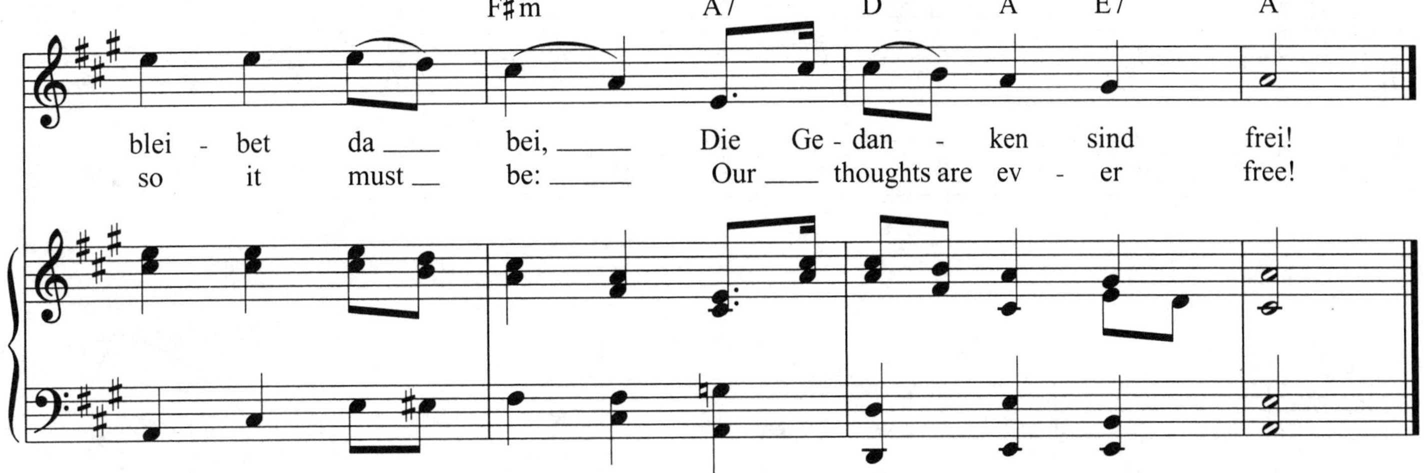
F♯m
A7
D
A
E7
A
blei - bet da bei, Die Ge - dan - ken sind frei!
so it must be: Our thoughts are ev - er free!

Ich denke was ich will,
Und was mich beglücket,
Doch alles in der Still,
Und wie es sich schicket.
Mein Wunsch und Begehren
Kann niemand verwehren,
Es bleibet dabei:
Die Gedanken sind frei!

Und sperrt, man mich ein
im finsteren Kerker,
Das alles sind rein
Vergebliche Werke;
Denn meine Gedanken
Zerreissen die Schranken
Und Mauern entzwei:
Die Gedanken sind frei!

So I think what I will,
And what does content me.
When all 'round is still,
Ideas are sent me.
My wishes, I try them,
No man can deny them.
And so it must be:
Our thoughts are ever free.

And if I am cast
Deep down in some prison,
It just cannot last,
For thoughts, once arisen,
Will fly through the air
To people everywhere,
And all will then see:
Our thoughts are ever free.

An die Freude
Ode To Joy

The "Ode to Joy" is sung in the finale of Beethoven's 9th Symphony — the "choral symphony."

Original German Poem by George Friedrich Schiller
English Paraphrase by Jerry Silverman
Music by Ludwig van Beethoven (adapted)

D A7 D A7 D
Freu - de, schön - er Göt - ter fun - ken, Toch - ter aus E -
Sing of joy from gods de - scend - ed, Daugh - ter of E -
A D A7
ly - si - um, wir be - tre - ten feu - er - trun - ken,
ly - si - um, Joy by love and hope at - ten - ded,
D A7 D A7 D A7 D
Himm - lisch - e, dein Heil - ig - thum. Dein - e zau - ber
Heav - en is your fair king - dom. For your mag - ic,

A7 D A7 D F#7 Bm E A D
bin - den wie - der, Was die Mo - de strengt get - heilt, Al -
like no oth - er's Re - u - nites us from on high. And
A7 D A7 D A7 D
le Men - schen werd - en Brü - der, wo dein sanf - te
all man - kind shall be broth - ers, Where your gen - tle
A7 D Dsus4 D Gsus4 G
Flü - gel weilt. Al - le Mensch - en, al - le Mensch - en werd - en
wings do fly. And all man - kind, and all man - kind will be
Em D A7 D
Brü der wo dein sanf - ter Flü - gel weilt
broth ers where your gen - tle wings do fly.

Es klappert die Mühle
The Mill Is A-Clanking

D A7 D
Es klap - pert die Müh - le am rausch - en - den Bach: Klipp, klapp. Bei
The mill is a clank - ing a - long - side the stream: Clip, clop. The
A7 D
Tag und bei Nacht ist der Mül - ler stets wach: Klipp, klapp. Er
mil - ler works hard and has no time to dream: Clip, clop. He
B7 Em A7
macht uns das Korn zu den kräft - ig - en Brot, Und hab - en wir sol - ches so
chang - es the grain in - to won - der - ful bread, And there is e - nough, so we
D A7 D
hat's kein - e Not: Klipp, klapp, klipp, klapp, klipp, klapp.
all can be fed: Clip, clop, clip, clop, clip, clop.

Flink laufen die Räder und drehen den Stein:
  Klipp, klapp.
Und mahlen den Weizen zu Mahl uns so fein:
  Klipp, klapp.
Der Bäcker dann Zwieback und Kuchen draus bäckt,
Der immer den Kindern besonders gut schmekt:
  Klipp, klapp, klipp, klapp, klipp klapp.

Wenn reichliche Körner das Ackerfeld trägt:
  Klipp, klapp.
Die Mühle dann flink ihre Räder bewegt:
  Klipp, klapp.
Und schenkt uns der Himmel nur immerdar Brot,
So sind wir geborgen und leiden nicht Not:
  Klipp, klapp, klipp, klapp, klipp, klapp.

The wheels turn so quickly, the stones grind away:
  Clip, clop.
They grind up the wheat into flour each day:
  Clip, clop.
The baker all sorts of delicious things bakes,
For children like biscuits and cookies and cakes:
  Clip, clop, clip, clop, clip, clop.

When harvests of plenty are brought in the fall:
  Clip, clop.
It's then that the mill wheels turn fastest of
  Clip, clop.
For heaven does always provide us with bread,
And we are protected from sorrow and need:
  Clip, clop, clip, clop, clip, clop.

Wir reisen noch Amerikâ
We Are Traveling To America

In 1830 Samuel Friedrich Sautter, a schoolmaster in Wurttemberg, Germany, wrote this song, which he included in his 1845 publication *Collected Poems of a Poor Village Schoolmaster.* Over the years it has achieved the status of a true folk song, with many variant versions. It found its way into Pennsylvania Dutch country, where it is sung to this day.

A Adim E7
Jetzt is di Zeit un Schtun - de dâ, Wir reis - en
To - day's the day and now's the hour, we tra - vel
A B7 E7 A E7
noch A - me - ri - kâ; D'r Wâj - je schteht schun fa d'r
to A - me - ri - ca; The wa - gon is pre - pared to
A D Bm E7sus4 E7 A
Dier, Mit Weib un Kin - ner zie - jen wir.
start, With wife and chil - dren we de - part.

Di Ferde sin schun eingeschpannt
Un alle die mit mir verwandt;
Di Ferde sin schun eingeschpannt,
Reich mir zum letschtenmâl di Hand.

Ach Freinde, weinet nicht so sehr
Wir sehen einander jetzt nimmermehr,
Ach Freinde, weinet nicht so sehr
Wir sehen einander nimmermehr.

Un wenn das Schiff aus dem Hâfen schwimmt
Do warren Lieder angeschtimmt,
Un wenn das Schiff aus dem Hâfen schwimmt
Do warren Lieder angeschtimmt.

Wir firchten keinen Wasserfall
Un dencken Gott ist iwwerall,
Wir firchten keinen Wasserfall
Un dencken Gott is iwwerrall.

Un kommen wir noch Baldimor
Do schtrecken wir di Hende vor,
Un rufen aus, "Victoriâ,
Jetzt sin wir in Amerikâ."

The horses are hitched up in place,
There's many a familiar face.
The horses are hitched up in place,
Reach out your hand in last embrace.

Dear friends, don't cry and don't complain,
We'll never see you all again.
Dear friends, don't cry and don't complain,
We'll never see you all again.

And as the ship sails out to sea,
We sing our songs so heartily.
And as the ship sails out to sea,
We sing our songs so heartily.

The stormy seas we do not fear,
Because we know our God is near.
The stormy seas we do not fear,
Because we know our God is near.

And when we come to Baltimore,
We raise our hands and loudly roar.
And then cry out, *"Victoria,*
Now we are in America."

Lied vom Mississippi
Mississippi Song

Only the text of this enthusiastic song has come down to us, accompanied by the vague indication, "1844 - Nach einer Negermelodie" (to a Negro melody). In seeking to find an appropriate tune that would do justice to the rhythmic bounce of the text, "The Patriotic Diggers" (which dates from the War of 1812) seemed a perfect fit, although it is not a "Negro melody."

Music by Samuel Woodworth
The Patriotic Diggers
Adapted by Jerry Silverman

G
D7
Brü - der laßt uns froh Jetzt das Glas er - he - ben,
Bro - thers, in our joy Let us lift our glass - es,
Am7
D7
G
Denn wir kön - nen frei. Nur im Aus - land le - ben.
For we're liv - ing here, And we need no pass - es.
Em
G
A7
D
Am
Am7
Kön - nen oh - ne Paß Üb - er - all spa - zier - en, Oh - ne Po - li -
In this for - eign land Ev - 'ry - where we're brows - ing, Nev - er do po -

D7
G
D7
G
zei
Täg-lich kom-mer - sier - en
Hier am Mis - sis - sip - pi.
lice
Stop us from ca - rous-ing
On the Mis - sis - sip - pi.

Freies Denken gilt
So wie freies Sprechen,
Nirgend, nirgend hier
Für ein Staatsverbrechen.
Hier macht kein Gendarm
Jemals uns Bedrängnis,
Und kein Bettelvogt
Führt uns ins Gefängnis
  Hier am Mississippi.

Our thoughts are free,
Freedom of expression.
Nowhere, nowhere here
Political repression.
Here there's no *gendarme*
That will give us trouble.
Here no bailiff leads us
To prison on the double -
  On the Mississippi.

Adel, Ordenskram,
Titel, Räng und Stände,
Und solch dummes Zeug,
Hat allhie ein Ende.
Hier darf nie ein Pfaff
Mit der Höll uns plagen,
Nie ein Jesuit
Uns die Ruh verjagen
  Hier am Mississippi.

Nobles, medal-junk,
Title, rank and standing,
And such stupid stuff,
Here does find its ending.
Here there are no priests
Threatening hell to curb us,
And no Jesuits
Are here to disturb us -
  On the Mississippi.

Früher lebten wir
Gleichsam nur zur Strafe,
Und man schor auch uns
Eben wie die Schafe.
Brüder, laßt uns drum
Singen, trinken, tanzen!
Keiner darf und kann
Hier uns je kuranzen,
  Hier am Mississippi.

Formerly we lived
Lives of constant fearing,
And we were like sheep
Led unto the shearing.
Brothers, let us go
Where our fortunes land us.
Singing, drinking, dancing,
None to reprimand us -
  On the Mississippi.

Michel, baue nicht
Ferner deine Saaten
Fürs Beamtenheer
Und die Herrn Soldaten!
Michel, faß ein Herz,
Endlich auszuwandern:
Hier gehörst du dir,
Dort nur stets den andern,
  Hier am Mississippi.

Michael, do not sow
Your seeds anymore now,
For the bureaucrats
And the men of war now.
Michael, listen here -
Leave with all your brothers.
Here you're your own man,
There you are another's -
  On the Mississippi.

Heil dir, Columbus
Hail To Thee, Columbus

After the political upheaval of 1848, thousands of disappointed Germans left their homeland for America. The best-known song among these people was this so-called "Columbus Song." The figure of Christopher Columbus assumed the stature of a patron saint and religious symbol.

A D E7 A E B7 E7
Heil dir, Co - lum - bus, sei ge - prie - sen, Sei hoch ge - ehrt in
Hail thee, Co - lum - bus, glo - ry to you, Hon - ored for all e -
A F♯m6 Esus4 E7 A D E7 A
E - wig - keit! Du hast mir den Weg ge - wie - sen,
ter - ni - ty! Thou hast shown me what I must do
E B7 G♯m C♯m F♯m B9 E E7 A A7
Der mich von har - ter Dienst - bar - keit Er - ret - tet hat, wenn
To flee from hard - est sla - ver - y. You res - cued me, I

D
D♯dim
E
A
E7
A
man es wagt, Und sein - em Va - ter land ent - sagt.
took my stand, And did re - nounce my fath - er - land.

Hier ist der Mensch an nichts gebunden,
Was er erwirbt, gehört auch sein,
Die Steuern sind noch nicht erfunden,
Die unser Leben machen zur Pein.
Wer redlich schafft, der hat sein Brot,
Er leid't kein Mangel und kein' Not.

Here may a man live life contented,
And he can keep what he does gain.
Taxes have not yet been invented,
That cause our life such constant pain.
The man that works will have his bread,
He'll have no lack and know no need.

Nun ist die Scheidestunde
Now Is The Parting Hour

Bremen was a major port of departure for German and other emigrants. This song, published in Berlin in 1855, is but one of many that takes a last look at Bremen before departing for the unknown.

And when we come to Bremen town,
Straight to an inn we sit us down.
And there we drink a flask of wine,
Leave Switzerland and Germany behind.

C
G7
Ach, wie vie - le schön - e Sach - en Er - zählt man
Of A - me - ri - ca, they tell me Such pret - ty
C
aus ___ A - me - ri - ka. ___ Und dort - hin wol - len wir uns
things, _ with - out com - pare. ___ And we are go - ing, Oh so
G7
C
mach - en, Das schön - ste Le - ben hat man da.
quick - ly, For life is sure - ly bet - ter there.

Hier hat man täglich seine Not
Wohl um das liebe schwarze Brot.
Wohlauf zu leben hat man da
Im schönen Land Amerika.

Komm, wir wollen auf die Reise gehn,
Der liebe Gott wird uns beistehn,
Er wird uns schützen mit seiner Hand
Und wird uns führen ins gepriesene Land.

Und als wir kommen in Bremen an,
Da heißt es "Brüder tretet an
Fürchtet keinen Wasserfall,
Der liebe Gott ist überall."

Und als wir kommen nach Baltimore,
Da heben wir die Hand empor
Und rufen laut Viktoria,
Jetzt sind wir in Amerika.

In Amerika ist gut sein,
Da gibt's gutes Bier und roten Wein.
Der rote Wein, der schmeckt uns gut
Und macht uns allen frohen Mut.

Every day we have what we need here,
All you want of tasty dark bread.
And everything you'd want to succeed here -
America, you're way ahead.

Come, we're ready to make the journey,
And God will surely lend a hand.
Yes, He'll protect us and stay with us,
And lead us to that wondrous land.

And when we arrived in Bremen,
It was then, "Brothers get on board,
And do not be afraid of the ocean -
Just put your faith all in the Lord."

And when we come to Baltimore,
We raise our hands and loudly roar.
And then cry out, *Viktoria,*
Now we are in America."

In America things are fine,
Here they have good beer and red wine.
The red wine, it tastes so good,
And it puts us in a happy mood.

Auf der Cimbria
On Board The Cimbria

The *Cimbria,* an emigrant ship, collided with the British steamer *Sultan* in the fog near Borkum Island, off the German coast, on January 19, 1883. It sank rapidly, with a loss of life of 420 people. On board, and among the victims, were two brothers from the town of Espa in Hesse. The wife of the pastor of Espa, Frau Schmitborn, was so moved by the fate of her neighbor's two sons that she quickly composed the text, which was then set to a simple tune by the pastor's serving girl. This tragic tale captured the popular imagination and was soon widely sung.

C
G7
C
Zwei Brü - der woll - ten wan- dern wohl nach A - me - ri - ka, Sie
Two bro - thers wished to wan- der all to A - me - ri - ca, They
F
G7
C
zo - gen mit viel an - dern wohl auf der Cim - bri - a.
went with man - y oth - ers on board the Cim - bri - a.

Der erste Tag war helle,
Dann stieg ein Nebel auf;
Die schiffer fuhren langsam
Den vorgeschriebnen Lauf.

Doch plötzlich sah man's
blinken
Zur Seit' ein helles Licht!
Ihr Lieben, wir versinken,
"Die *Cimbria,* sie bricht."

Der Bruder sprach zum
andern:
Wenn du gerettet wirst,
"So ziehe in die Heimat
Und grüsse sie von mir!"

The first day it was sunny,
But then a cloud appeared.
The ships proceeded slowly,
As on their course they
steered.

And then we saw a blinking,
A bright light in the gloom.
Dear friends, I fear we're
sinking,
The *Cimbria* is doomed.

Then brother spoke to brother,
"When you will rescued be,
Return unto our homeland,
And greet them all for me."

Der Bruder aber schweiget,
Sein Mund war schon
verstummt,
Da zogen die Gewässer
Die beiden in den Grund.

Nun hat's ein End mit diesen,
Die hier versunken sind.
Lebe vohl, du mein
Feinsliebchen,
Lebe wohl, auf Wiedersehen!

The brother, he was silent,
His mouth, it spoke no more,
For soon beneath the waters
Both sank forevermore.

So there's an end to those two
That drowned beneath the
main.
Live well, my dearest sweet -
heart,
Live well, *auf wiedersehen.*

CIMBRIA

Die Moorsoldaten
The Peat-Bog Soldiers

This song was written by prisoners in the Börgermoor concentration camp (in the northwest corner of Germany, near the Dutch frontier) in 1933. It was actually sung by the prisoners on their way to and from work. Finally, the emphasis that they put on the last stanza caused the Nazis to forbid the singing of the song entirely.

Words by Johann Esser
and Wolfgang Langhoff

Music by Rudi Goguel

Em B7 Em B7 Em B7 Em Em7 Am Am6 Em
Wo - hin auch das Au - ge blick - et, Moor und Hei - de
Far and wide as the eye can wan - der, Heath and bog are
Am6 B7 Em G G/F♯ G/E D7 G G/F♯ G/E G/D
rings - her - um. Vo - gel - sang uns nicht er - quick - et,
ev - 'ry - where. Not a bird sings out to cheer us,
Chorus
Am6 Em A♯dim B7sus4 B7 Em D7 G
Eich - en steh - en kalt und krumm. Wir sind die Moor - sol -
Oaks are stand - ing gaunt and bare. We are the peat - bog

D D♯dim Em Am6 B7sus4 B7 Em D7 Em
1. 2.
da - ten, Und zie - hen mit dem Spa - ten ins Moor. Wir Moor.
sol - diers,We're march - ing with our spades to the bog. We bog.

Hier in dieser öden Heide
ist das Lager aufgebaut,
wo wir fern von jeder Freude
hinter Stacheldraht verstaut. *(Chorus)*

Here in dreary desolation,
We're behind the prison wall.
Far from every consolation,
Barbed wire does surround us all. *(Chorus)*

Morgens ziehen die Kolonnen
in das Moor zur Arbeit hin.
Graben bei dem Brand der Sonnen,
doch zur Heimat steht der sinn. *(Chorus)*

Mornings we're marched out in one line,
On the moorland to our toil;
Digging under burning sunshine,
Thinking of our native soil. *(Chorus)*

Heimwärts, heimwärts jeder sehnet
sich zu Eltern, Weib und Kind.
Manche Brust ein Seufzer dehnet,
weil wir hier gefangen sind. *(Chorus)*

Homeward, homeward, each is yearning
For his parents, child and wife.
In each breast a sigh is burning -
We're imprisoned here for life. *(Chorus)*

Auf und nieder gehn die Posten,
keiner, keiner kann hindurch,
Flucht wird nur das Leben kosten!
Vierfach ist umzäunt die Burg. *(Chorus)*

Up and down the guards are pacing,
No one can escape this place.
Flight would mean a sure death facing,
Four-fold 'round the guards do pace. *(Chorus)*

Doch für uns gibt es kein Klagen,
ewig kann's nicht Winter sein.
Einmal werden froh wir sagen:
Heimat, du bist wieder mein.

But for us there is no complaining,
Winter one day will be past.
One day, free, we'll be exclaiming:
"Homeland, you are mine at last!"

(Final Chorus)

Dann ziehn die Moorsoldaten
nicht mehr mit dem Spaten
ins Moor.

(Final Chorus)

Then will the peat-bog soldiers
March no more with their spades
To the bog.

MEL BAY

Great Music at Your Fingertips